TRAINING FOR SPEED
AND ENDURANCE

Training for speed and endurance

Edited by
Peter Reaburn and David Jenkins

ALLEN & UNWIN

First published in 1996 by
Allen & Unwin Pty Ltd
9 Atchison Street, St Leonards, NSW 2065 Australia
Phone: (61 2) 9901 4088
Fax: (61 2) 9906 2218
E-mail: 100252.103@compuserve.com

National Library of Australia
Cataloguing-in-Publication entry:

Training for speed and endurance.

Includes index.
ISBN 1 86448 120 X.

1. Physical education and training. I. Jenkins, David, 1961– .
II. Reaburn, Peter, 1955– .

613.711

Set in 11.5/13.5 pt Garamond by DOCUPRO, Sydney
Printed by Southwood Press, Australia

10 9 8 7 6 5 4 3 2 1

Contents

Tables

Figures

About the authors

The editors

David Jenkins PhD: Lecturer in Exercise Physiology within the Department of Human Movement Studies at The University of Queensland. Has been the senior scientific consultant to the Australian Rugby Football Union (ARFU) and Australian Institute of Sport (Rugby) since 1988.

Peter Reaburn PhD: Lecturer in Exercise Physiology within the Department of Human Movement Studies at The University of Queensland. Member, National Coaching Panel, AUSSI Masters Swimming. World-ranked 1500m freestyle (35–39 years).

Invited authors

Angie Calder MA (Hons): Recovery Training Coordinator, Australian Institute of Sport. Invited speaker at numerous international coaching conferences and consultant to several high-profile professional and representative sporting teams.

Greg Cox BHMS, Grad.Dip.Nutr.Diet: Holder of the Berrivale Orchards Nutrition Fellowship at the Australian Institute of Sport (1995). Is actively involved in Surf Lifesaving.

Michael Dalgleish B.App.Sci.(Phty), BHMS: Physiotherapist to the Australian Women's Hockey Team. Consultant to the Australian Institute of Sport and Queensland Academy of Sport. Physiotherapy Director to the Brisbane Broncos Rugby League team.

Brian Dawson PhD: Senior Lecturer, The University of Western Australia and Fitness Coach, West Coast Eagles (AFL) since 1988.

Holly Frail BSc, Grad.Dip.Nutr.Diet: Sports dietitian and consultant to the Australian and Queensland Rugby Unions, Brisbane Broncos Rugby League team, Australian Diving team and Queensland Academy of Sport.

Matt Freke Dip. Phty, M.Phty St: Consultant to the Queensland Academy of Sport. Physiotherapy Director to the Crushers Rugby League team.

Kerry Leech BSc, Grad.Dip.Diet: Sports dietitian and consultant to Australian Institute of Sport (Qld), Queensland Academy of Sport, Australian and Queensland Netball teams and Australian Softball.

Craig Maskiell BHMS (Hons): Fitness adviser to the Brisbane Bears Australian Rules team, Member of the Australian Open Triathlon team (1991).

Lachlan Penfold BHMS, CSCS: Conditioning consultant in charge of the Queensland Rugby Union team, the Brisbane Bandits (Baseball) team, Australian Baseball squad and Australian Institute of Sport (Softball).

Acknowledgments

The editors gratefully acknowledge the invaluable assistance of Judith Jenkins (for proofreading the original script) and Debbie Noon (for producing the diagrams).

Preface

Elite athletes and coaches are increasingly turning to sports science in order to gain an extra edge over their competitors. In order to optimise speed and endurance development for competition, these coaches and athletes need a good understanding of the principles of exercise physiology and how these concepts can be used to develop the most effective training programs. However, just as there exists a gap between elite sport and the general sporting community, there also exists a gap between sports science and coaches and athletes. *Training for speed and endurance* aims to bridge this gap by bringing together sports scientists who not only work with elite athletes but are at the cutting edge of sports science. We have synthesised the latest findings from sports science and present them in a way that is easily understood by coaches and athletes at all levels.

Training for speed and endurance contains chapters on state-of-the-art training techniques for developing speed and endurance in the individual athlete, as well as the team player. As sports scientists, we recognise the importance of organising the training year carefully in order to maximise an athlete's development, and have included a chapter on periodisation for the speed and endurance athlete as well as for the team player. Astute coaches and athletes also appreciate the need to maximise recovery, minimise and prevent injuries, and adopt nutritional practices that maximise both recovery and sports performance. *Training for speed and endurance* has brought together Australia's leading practitioners in all these fields.

As editors, we have made every attempt to make this book as informative and practical as possible. We hope our readers will gain that edge over their competitors they have been looking for.

Peter Reaburn and David Jenkins

1

Introduction to exercise physiology

Dr David Jenkins and Dr Peter Reaburn

This chapter will review some of the principles of physiology upon which our understanding of speed and endurance training methods are based. An explanation of the energy systems is followed by a review of the muscle fibres which athletes rely upon to compete. These two concepts are closely linked by the intensity and duration of exercise and are therefore central to implementing an effective training program. Finally, the concepts of maximal oxygen uptake and the anaerobic threshold are explained in the context of endurance training and testing.

THE ENERGY SYSTEMS

Muscles require energy to contract. Most physiological events such as exercise, growth and repair depend upon energy stored in a chemical compound called adenosine tri-phosphate (ATP) (see Figure 1.1).

Resting levels of muscle ATP are relatively small. In fact, although we only store approximately 100g of ATP in our entire muscular system over 50kg of ATP will be used during a marathon. Thus our bodies must continually remake or *resynthesise* ATP to sustain exercise. This is achieved by the

Figure 1.1: Energy release from ATP by the enzyme ATPase

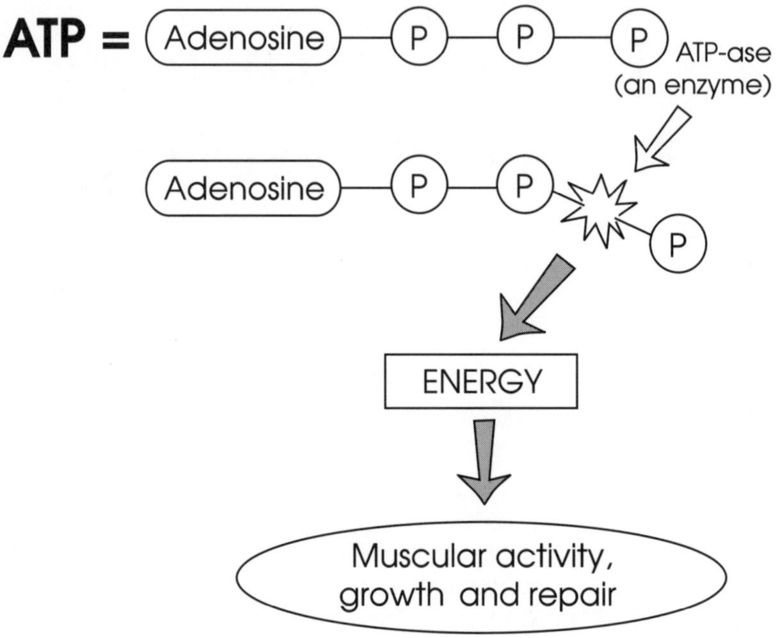

transfer of the chemical energy found in fats, carbohydrates and proteins to rebuild the ATP molecule (see Figure 1.2).

Training, be it sprint, endurance, interval or resistance (weights), does not increase our resting ATP concentrations. Instead, training improves our ability to maintain ATP *resynthesis*. Provided we can produce ATP at the same rate it is needed by the muscles for contraction, we can delay the onset of fatigue. As soon as we fail to produce ATP at the rate at which we are using it, fatigue sets in. Thus, the maintenance of ATP levels within muscle tissue is the primary goal of athletic training. Our ability to resynthesise ATP within the muscle cells in order to support continued exercise relies upon three energy systems:

- Creatine phosphate (CrP) system
- 'Anaerobic' glycolysis or lactic acid system
- Aerobic or oxygen system

Before we examine each of the systems in detail, two points should be considered. First, it is important to appreciate that

Figure 1.2: Energy from carbohydrate, fat, protein and creatine phosphate is used to resynthesise ATP from ADP (adenosine di-phosphate) and P (phosphate). The ATP is then used for muscle contraction

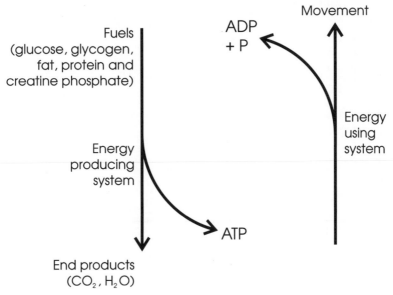

all three energy systems can operate at the same time within the same muscle cell. For example, all three energy systems, including the aerobic system, are used simultaneously at the onset of sprint exercise (see Figure 1.3). The major feature that distinguishes these energy systems is the speed at which they function and the total amount of ATP resynthesised by each series of chemical reactions.

While Figure 1.3 is the classic diagram used to identify which energy systems are used in specific events, it does assume maximal effort from time zero. Figure 1.4 is another model best used when examining team players who may go easy at the start of a game but have to sprint at various intensities throughout the game. Figure 1.4 shows that the greater the intensity of effort, the greater the rate of ATP turnover, the greater the reliance on anaerobic glycolysis and creatine phosphate.

The second important point is that the 'trigger' which initiates the chemical reactions necessary for the transfer of

3

Figure 1.3: Relative contribution of the three energy systems as a function of time. This graph makes the assumption that exercise intensity is maximal from time zero

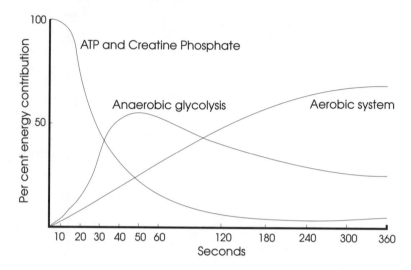

Figure 1.4: Energy needed to perform various power outputs, expressed as a percentage of VO₂max, and the relative contribution of aerobic metabolism, anaerobic glycolysis and ATP/CrP

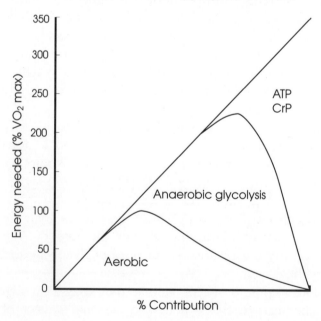

energy from fats, carbohydrates and proteins for ATP resynthesis is a *decrease* in a cell's ATP concentration. As soon as resting ATP levels fall (which has to occur when muscles contract), the chemical reactions immediately begin.

CREATINE PHOSPHATE SYSTEM

Creatine phosphate (CrP) is a stored chemical which in practical terms is similar to ATP. When an enzyme (which is a substance responsible for controlling chemical reactions) splits creatine from phosphate, energy is released and transferred for ATP resynthesis (see Figure 1.5). Energy from the splitting of CrP is provided very quickly and requires only one anaerobic chemical reaction (i.e. a reaction which is not dependent on oxygen).

Muscle cells have relatively low stores of CrP and we normally deplete our reserves within seconds of beginning a sprint. CrP will then only be resynthesised during very low intensity exercise or complete rest. Moreover, it may take several minutes of continual oxygen supply to the muscles for CrP to return to pre-exercise levels. This is why sprinters should have long recovery bouts between sprints when training.

Because of the speed with which CrP can 'donate' energy to remake ATP, sprint and power athletes and team players requiring bursts of explosive speed are particularly dependent on their CrP stores. There is enormous current scientific and commercial interest in 'creatine loading' (through dietary supplementation of creatine compounds such as 'Ergomax') which has been shown by some scientists to increase resting CrP levels and improve high intensity exercise performance.

The question as to whether sprint training alone can increase resting CrP levels is somewhat debatable. While some studies have shown an increase in CrP levels, most have not. What is important is that we can train the rate at which CrP is broken down to provide energy to rebuild ATP which in turn is available to support the contraction of our muscles during high intensity exercise.

Figure 1.5: Energy and phosphate (P), derived from splitting creatine phosphate (CrP), are used to resynthesise ATP from ADP and P

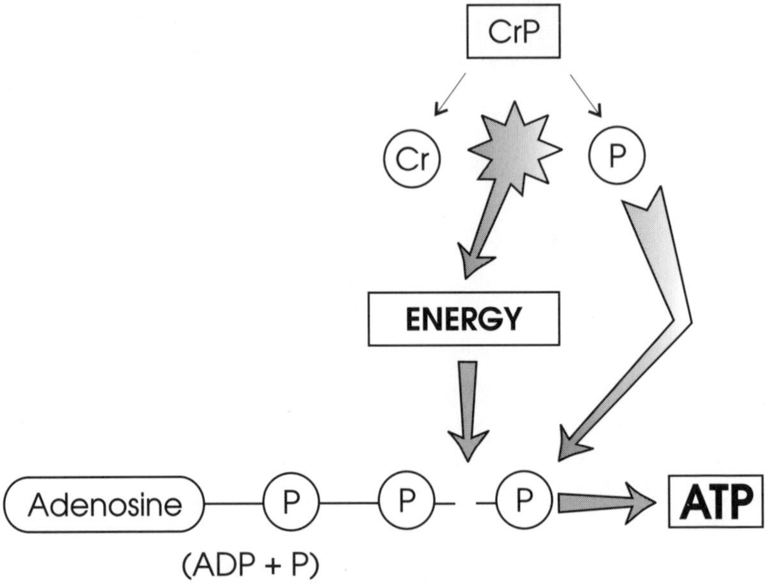

ANAEROBIC GLYCOLYSIS OR LACTIC ACID SYSTEM

Anaerobic glycolysis, which is sometimes referred to as the lactic acid system, relies upon 13 chemical reactions to convert glycogen (stored carbohydrate) to lactic acid. This system can only use carbohydrate (glucose or glycogen) and not fat or protein, both of which can only be used with oxygen. Whereas glycogen is the fuel, lactic acid is the end product of anaerobic glycolysis. The energy which is released during the conversion from glycogen to lactic acid is again transferred to remake ATP.

Compared with the single chemical reaction needed to liberate energy from CrP, it is not surprising that the 13 steps of anaerobic glycolysis take longer to make the energy available. However, this pathway of reactions is still faster than the series of reactions which make energy available from the aerobic system. This is why sprinters also depend upon anaerobic glycolysis to supplement their limited CrP reserves during sprinting. The longer the sprint (>20 seconds), the greater the reliance on anaerobic glycolysis to provide energy.

Lactic acid production and recovery

Although anaerobic glycolysis provides quick energy, lactic acid can accumulate within the muscles. To a limited extent, muscles can cope with a mild accumulation of acid. However, if lactic acid production is great (as it is during longer sprints), acidity (acidosis) increases. As will be discussed in more detail in Chapter 2, acidosis is believed to be a major cause of fatigue during sprint exercise, particularly in events over 30 seconds in duration. Acidosis will generally be reduced to normal levels within approximately 30 minutes of recovery, depending on the intensity and duration of the sprint and the *type* of recovery an athlete elects to undertake (active or passive). An active recovery (a light jog, swim or ride) will remove the acid faster than complete rest.

Interestingly, it is the aerobic system which allows removal of the lactic acid and again helps the muscle to return to normal. Thus, as with the remaking of CrP, recovery of the muscle from a build-up of lactic acid is oxygen-dependent. One further point related to lactic acid and recovery is that muscle soreness is now known to be caused by factors completely independent of lactic acid accumulation. Contrary to earlier beliefs, which linked lactic acidosis with the soreness which so often persists for several days following hard exercise, it is now accepted that microscopic structural damage to the muscle cells is responsible for the pain.

As will be explained in Chapter 2, *sprint* training improves an athlete's ability to use anaerobic glycolysis. A number of favourable changes such as improved ability to produce lactic acid more quickly and to tolerate it better can occur and these allow the trained sprinter to derive energy quickly and to cope with an increased production of lactic acid.

AEROBIC OR OXYGEN ENERGY SYSTEM

The aerobic system, also known as the oxygen energy system, can only function when oxygen is supplied to the muscles. When oxygen is available, fat, carbohydrate and protein can be broken down inside a cell structure called the mitochondrial reticulum (network). Aerobic chemical reactions are relatively slow compared to those in the glycolytic pathway. However, considerably more energy becomes available aerobically than through either of the two anaerobic energy pathways. The slower rate of ATP resynthesis is due to the necessary transfer of fuel between different compartments in the cell. The aerobic system also depends upon oxygen delivery from the lungs, which is governed by blood flow from the heart, to the lungs, back to the heart and then to the muscles. All these processes take time—time the sprinter simply does not have but the endurance athlete does.

Those who derive most benefit from the aerobic system are distance athletes. Endurance training not only improves the body's ability to deliver oxygen to the active muscles but it also enhances the capacity of the muscles to use oxygen within their mitochondria. Furthermore, team players who need to recover between sprints or efforts need an efficient aerobic system to remove lactic acid and enhance recovery. Chapter 3 reviews how endurance training improves the function of the aerobic system.

In summary, the energy systems try to maintain adequate levels of ATP in order to allow muscle contraction to keep taking place. Table 1.1 summarises each of the energy systems and their characteristics.

TYPES OF MUSCLE FIBRES

Muscles are specialised structures which allow force to be generated. Skeletal muscle is generally considered to be made up of the following three fibre types:

Table 1.1: Summary of the energy systems		
ATP-PC (phosphagen) system	**Anaerobic glycolysis or lactic acid system**	**Aerobic or oxygen system**
Anaerobic	Anaerobic	Aerobic
Very rapid	Rapid	Slow
Chemical fuel: PC	Fuel: glycogen	Fuels: glycogen, fats, protein
Very limited ATP production	Limited ATP production	Unlimited ATP production
Muscular stores limited	By-product, lactic acid, causes muscular fatigue	No fatiguing by-products
Primary use with sprint or any high-power, short duration activity up to 20 seconds	Primary use in intense activities of 30 sec. to 2 mins duration	Primary use in endurance or long-duration activities

- Type I (slow twitch or 'red' fibres)
- Type IIa (fast oxidative fibres)
- Type IIb (fast twitch or 'white' fibres)

Individual differences in fibre type

Different skeletal muscles, such as the biceps in the arm or the gastrocnemius in the calf, contain differing numbers (and sizes) of fibres. They also differ in their proportions of Type I and Type II fibres. For example, whereas for most people the quadriceps and gastrocnemius muscles are made up of approximately 50% Type I and 50% Type II fibres, the soleus in the calf and EDL (extensor digitalis longus) muscle in the foot contain mostly Type I and Type II muscle fibres, respectively. These distributions probably reflect the type of exercise each muscle group has been expected to perform over the millions of years we have evolved. The soleus muscle has probably always been involved in low intensity, postural work whereas the EDL has been primarily responsible for faster movements of shorter duration.

While most of us conform to fairly common distribution patterns (50% slow and 50% fast muscle fibres), individual differences do exist both in the number of fibres within each muscle group and the relative distribution of Types I and II, particularly within 'mixed' muscles such as the quadriceps

9

Figure 1.6: Percentage of slow twitch (Type I) fibres sampled from the gastrocnemius muscle of various elite athletes. The percentage Type I fibres in an untrained population is also shown

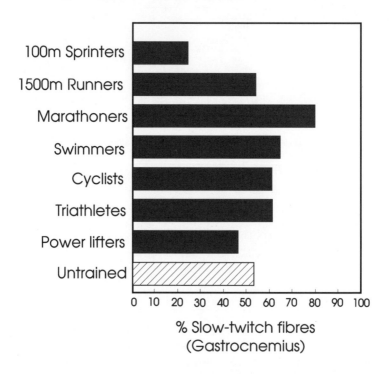

and gastrocnemius groups. Most scientific evidence suggests that both the *number* and *type* of muscle fibres are genetically fixed at birth. This is why elite endurance athletes and elite sprinters are born rather than made. However, training will allow an athlete to work within these genetic constraints. An examination of the specific characteristics of these three fibres and how each can be influenced by training will now be discussed. Figure 1.6 shows the average distribution of fibre types in the gastrocnemius according to activity at the elite level.

Table 1.2 summarises the key characteristics of each of the three fibre types. The following discussion examines each fibre type in turn and the associated implications for speed and endurance training.

Table 1.2: Characteristics of fibre types

Characteristics	Slow (Type I)	Fast (Type II)	
		IIa	IIb
Contractile speed	slow	fast	fast
Size	small	large	large
Force produced	low	high	high
Fatiguability	slight	great	great
Mitochondria	many	many	few
Mitochondrial enzyme activity	great	great	slight
Glycogen stores	slight	great	great
Glycolytic capacity	slight	great	great
Capillaries	many	moderate	few
Nerve size	small	large	large
Nerve conduction velocity	slow	fast	fast
% in typical leg muscles	45	38	16
% in leg muscles of distance runner	80	14	5
% in leg muscles of sprinter	23	48	28

TYPE I MUSCLE FIBRES

Type I or slow twitch fibres are relatively slow to contract but also slow to fatigue. They are smaller in size than the Type II fibres which means they possess less contractile proteins and are therefore weaker.

Type I fibres and energy production

Type I fibres rely heavily, though not exclusively, upon *aerobic* metabolism to produce ATP. To achieve this, they are richly served by capillaries (the smallest blood vessels in tissue) and have an extensive mitochondrial reticulum to generate aerobic energy using oxygen. Remember that aerobic metabolism within a cell can only occur inside the mitochondrial reticulum. While Type I fibres are best suited to aerobic metabolism, they are nonetheless capable of anaerobic metabolism (albeit at a lower rate than the Type II fibres). Anaerobic metabolism becomes more important when the rate of ATP resynthesis has to meet a high ATP demand—as in sprint exercise.

The red colour associated with Type I fibres is due to both the high number of capillaries and the high density of iron-based enzymes and chemicals in the mitochondrial reticulum. It is also worth noting that because fat can only be burned in the mitochondrial reticulum and Type I fibres have an extensive mitochondrial reticulum, these slow twitch fibres have a high capacity for burning fat. Endurance athletes take particular advantage of this. By maximising the burning of fat as a fuel, carbohydrate stores can be spared and an athlete can delay 'hitting the wall' (a term used by athletes to describe the onset of glycogen depletion).

Elite endurance athletes (and indeed all athletes who find long-distance activities fairly easy), typically have a relatively high proportion of Type I fibres in muscles such as the quadriceps (thigh) and gastrocnemius (calf). While training will certainly improve almost any athlete's ability to undertake endurance exercise, research has shown that it is not possible to increase their genetically determined *number* of Type I fibres (either through growing new fibres or at the expense of converted Type II fibres).

TYPE II MUSCLE FIBRES (IIA AND IIB)

Type II muscle fibres, also known as 'fast twitch' or 'white' fibres, have two subgroups: a highly glycolytic white fibre (IIb) and a fibre which shares both glycolytic and aerobic capabilities (IIa). The Type II fibres are larger than the Type I fibres and possess a higher density of contractile proteins. Thus, they are capable of generating considerably more force, at a faster rate, than the Type I fibres. However, Type II fibres, and in particular Type IIb, fatigue more quickly and take longer to recover following high intensity exercise. This is partially due to the smaller number of capillaries present and consequent slower oxygen delivery.

The Type IIb fibres favour *anaerobic* glycolysis rather than aerobic metabolism to produce ATP. Instead of an extensive mitochondrial reticulum (which is more common in Type I fibres), Type IIb fibres have a greater number of contractile proteins (the structures in muscle capable of producing force rather than producing energy). This allows the fibres to generate more strength but at a cost of a poorer ability to sustain continued contraction. This is due, at least in part, to their producing more lactic acid which can fatigue a muscle. The white colour of the Type IIb fibres reflects both a relative absence of mitochondrial reticulum and a lower number of capillaries.

While Type IIa fibres are considered fast, they are more capable of undertaking *aerobic* metabolism than IIb fibres; they possess a more extensive mitochondrial reticulum and are positioned more closely to oxygen-delivering capillaries than the Type IIb fibres. Type IIa fibres are slightly smaller in diameter and are not as capable of quite the same force of contraction as Type IIb fibres. However, they are more resistant to fatigue than the larger Type IIb fibres.

Elite sprinters have higher proportions of Type II fibres than endurance athletes. Again, this seems to be genetically pre-determined. Research has shown, however, that it is possible to 'shift' between Type IIa and Type IIb fibres in response to specific training programs. For example, with a period of endurance training, an athlete will increase the number of Type IIa fibres at the expense of his/her Type IIb fibres.

Before leaving this section to consider how these fibre types are recruited (brought into action) during speed and endurance training or racing, it is worth remembering that the Type I and Type IIb fibres favour the aerobic and anaerobic energy systems respectively. However, endurance or sprint training will induce specific adaptations which improve the capabilities of particular fibres to cope better with new demands. For example, if a marathon runner were to complete eight weeks of sprint training, his/her muscles would improve the ability to produce energy through the two anaerobic energy systems.

The three muscle fibre types are recruited in a unique pattern during progressively harder exercise. This so-called principle of motor unit recruitment has enormous implications for both training and warming-up before training or competing.

MOTOR UNIT RECRUITMENT

The motor unit

A motor unit is collectively a nerve and those muscle fibres which the nerve stimulates. Because it is the nerve which determines the muscle fibres' speed of contraction, all muscle fibres in a particular motor unit will be of the same type. Thus, a fast nerve will control fast contracting (Type II) fibres, and a slow nerve will stimulate slow (Type I) fibres.

In response to training, the body coordinates movement in a remarkably efficient manner. That is, excessive involvement of motor units is avoided and only the minimum number of units is recruited to perform the exercise if we train with the correct technique. We therefore use the motor units that produce force to make us run, swim and cycle faster and not those that produce wasted movements.

The pattern of motor unit recruitment

Consider an athlete at a running track who has been asked to gradually increase her running speed (building up from a jog to an all-out sprint) over a distance of 800m. Figure 1.7 shows that at the start of the run, only some Type I motor units are active (since they can quite easily cope with the slow running speed). Moreover, we know that these motor units within her leg muscles are randomly recruited so that the fuel is shared across the entire muscle group and thus local depletion of glycogen in some motor units is prevented (this is not apparent from the diagram).

As her running speed increases further, a greater number of Type I fibres are recruited to meet the higher work rate. However, there will inevitably be a speed above which all the Type I fibres will collectively be unable to meet an increase in running speed. At this stage, Type IIa fibres are recruited to *assist* the Type I fibres. As before, the number of Type IIa motor units involved in the exercise task will continue to increase as her running speed becomes faster. When further increases in running speed can no longer be

Figure 1.7: Muscle fibres are recruited in order of size (Type I > IIa > IIb) during exercise of increasing intensity

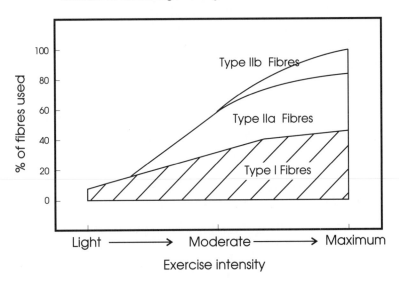

met by the recruitment of more Type IIa motor units, Type IIb motor units begin their contribution. They too increase their involvement as the athlete accelerates to top speed.

There are a couple of important aspects to this scenario. Firstly, this gradual recruitment of motor units will only occur during exercise which involves a progressive increase in speed or power output. During an all-out sprint, all units are recruited simultaneously at the onset of exercise. The second important point is that Type I fibres are involved in exercise of all intensities whereas Type IIa, and to a greater extent Type IIb, fibres only contribute to higher intensity exercise (where either force or speed is needed). It seems that some Type IIb units are only recruited at near maximal effort. This is known as 'the size principle of motor unit recruitment'; the smallest units (Type I) are recruited first and the larger Type II units are recruited last. If an athlete were asked to slow down gradually from an all-out sprint, taking another 800m to finally stop, the Type IIb motor units would cease their involvement first, then the Type IIa and finally, when stopped, the Type I units would cease to contract, following a 'first-in, last-out' principle.

Fibre recruitment

This pattern of motor unit recruitment has at least three implications for exercise and training. First, the intensity of an athlete's training must be specific. If athletes restrict their training to low intensity endurance exercise, the larger and more powerful Type II motor units will simply not be recruited and will remain untrained. Now this may not necessarily matter for the endurance athlete, but for the sprinter and team player, high intensity exercise is essential for adaptations to the larger motor units to occur. Second, interval (speed) training will recruit the more anaerobic Type IIb fibres and possibly convert them to the more aerobic Type IIa fibres. Third, for an athlete who needs to warm-up prior to high intensity exercise, failure to recruit the Type II fibres in the warm-up routine is likely to impair subsequent performance and also increase the risk of injury.

In summary, muscle fibre composition can help explain why some athletes are genetically designed to compete at the highest level in either sprint or endurance activities. Equally important, however, is recognising that we can, within certain genetic limitations, expect significant improvements in muscle function in response to training. Finally, the pattern of motor unit recruitment underlies many physiological events. Appreciating the implications of this phenomenon is fundamental to understanding the principles of training.

Let us now turn our attention to two factors that are important to both endurance athletes and team players who need to cover a lot of distance in a game and/or recover quickly between efforts—the concepts of maximal aerobic capacity (VO_2max) and anaerobic threshold.

MAXIMAL AEROBIC CAPACITY

Maximal aerobic capacity is defined as the maximal amount of oxygen that can be transported to, and consumed by, the working muscles in exercise. Maximal aerobic capacity or VO_2max is the same as the terms 'maximum oxygen consumption', 'maximal oxygen intake', 'maximal aerobic power' and 'maximum oxygen uptake'.

Measuring VO_2max

To measure VO_2max, one must know the volume (V) of oxygen (O_2) inspired and the volume expired. The difference between these two volumes is the amount of oxygen that has been taken up by the mitochondrial reticulum to produce energy in the working muscles. Testing and measuring oxygen consumption is a routine procedure in exercise laboratories, but requires highly sophisticated equipment and technical expertise. Fortunately, there are other methods of estimating VO_2max such as the Multistage Fitness Test ('Beep Test') available from the Australian Coaching Council or the University of Montreal Track Test (see 'Further Reading' at end of this chapter). The former test is great for team sports that shuttle up and back, the latter is designed for continuous running athletes.

Because oxygen is used by all body tissues, a larger individual will have a greater oxygen uptake than a smaller person both at rest and during exercise. In order to allow comparisons between individuals, oxygen uptake (litres/minute) is divided by body weight to produce figures in millilitres of oxygen per kilogram of body weight per minute (ml/kg/min).

Typical values

Normal resting oxygen uptake is approximately 3.5 ml/kg/min. During maximal exercise, this may increase 10 to 20 times depending on age, gender, and endurance fitness level (see Table 3.1 on page 45 for elite athlete values). Typical values for 17–20 year olds who do not exercise are 48 and 40ml/kg/min for men and women respectively. Men generally have higher values due to their larger muscle mass which can take up and use more oxygen. Women also tend to have smaller hearts and less oxygen-carrying capacity (haemoglobin) in their blood. Trained endurance athletes have extremely high values for VO_2max (60+ ml/kg/min), which means they have the capacity to use oxygen at a much higher rate than most other athletes. Thus, they can perform at a higher rate with less fatigue and generally for longer periods.

Variables affecting VO₂max

VO$_2$max is a function of three variables: maximal heart rate (MHR), maximal stroke volume (SV), and maximal arteriovenous oxygen difference (A-VO$_2$ diff.).

Maximal heart rate (MHR)

This is the maximum rate at which an individual's heart rate will beat, in beats per minute. It is generally determined as 220 – age ± 10 beats, but wide variations occur. In the research laboratory it is quite possible, for example, to find that two 18 year old cyclists (theoretical MHR = 202) have maximal heart rates at 216 and 180 respectively. As will be discussed in Chapter 3, it is critical that endurance athletes establish their MHR. Indeed, if they are involved in a number of activities (eg. triathlon) they will need to establish their MHR for each activity, since MHR in motivated athletes is a function of muscle mass and body position used in the sport. For example, a 20 year old triathlete's MHR for running might be 205, for cycling 190, and for swimming 185.

Maximal stroke volume

This is the maximum amount of blood pumped by the left ventricle of the heart with each beat. Normal resting stroke volume in untrained people is about 70ml of blood and in endurance-trained athletes is approximately 90ml. At maximal exercise, these values increase to 125ml in untrained subjects and up to 200ml in endurance-trained athletes. The higher stroke volume of endurance athletes is the major reason why they have lower resting and exercise heart rates. If both groups require the same volume of blood per minute to deliver oxygen to the working or resting muscles, and the athlete pumps more blood per beat, then it follows that the athlete's heart will beat at a lower rate. It also follows that for the same heart rate the athlete's heart will deliver more blood, hence more oxygen, to the working muscles.

Maximal arterio-venous oxygen difference
This is the maximal difference between the amount of oxygen in the arterial blood (that delivers oxygen to the muscles) and the amount of oxygen in the venous blood (that removes left-over oxygen from the muscles). The difference has been used to create aerobic energy within the mitochondrial reticulum, that is, it was consumed by the working muscles. Normal arterial oxygen content is 20ml O_2/100 ml blood during rest and exercise. Normal resting venous oxygen content is 15ml O_2/100ml blood, but this may decrease to 2–5ml O_2/100ml during maximal exercise.

Effects of training on VO₂max

Compared to an untrained person, an endurance-trained athlete has both a greater stroke volume and a greater arterio-venous oxygen difference. These result in a greater VO₂max. Sports science has shown that VO₂max is 75% heredity and 25% trainable. Endurance training leads to changes both at the heart (SV) and blood level, and at the muscle level.

Improved stroke volume is due to one or more of the following:

- The left ventricle hypertrophies (enlarges) internally, therefore more blood can be pumped per beat.
- With a slower resting heart rate, there is more time for the left ventricle to fill, therefore a greater volume is available to be pumped.
- There is greater elasticity of the cardiac muscle fibres, which allows a larger volume of blood to enter the heart and its chambers.
- There is improved strength of contraction in the cardiac muscle and therefore a greater amount of the blood is injected into the left ventricle for pumping to the muscles.

These changes account for about 50% of the improvement in VO_2 max with training. The other 50% occurs at the muscle level with changes in maximal arterio-venous oxygen difference. Some possible mechanisms to explain the larger maximal arterio-venous oxygen difference include:

- Improved myoglobin concentration, enhancing oxygen diffusion from blood to muscle.
- More capillaries for each fibre, so that more blood and oxygen are closer to the working fibre.
- Increased density of mitochondrial reticulum, the site of aerobic metabolism within the muscle.
- Increased concentration of the aerobic enzymes that generate the aerobic energy.

With all these factors improving aerobic capacity, we would expect VO_2max to be a good predictor of endurance performance. However, research has shown that VO_2max itself is not as good a predictor of performance as the percentage of VO_2max at which an athlete can work in a race. Obviously the higher the percentage the better the performance. This introduces the concept of the anaerobic threshold.

ANAEROBIC THRESHOLD

Anaerobic threshold is defined as that point where the energy demands of exercise cannot be met totally by available aerobic sources and at which an increase in anaerobic metabolism occurs. This increase in anaerobic metabolism is reflected by an increase in blood lactic acid. As noted earlier, an accumulation of lactic acid in the muscle has negative effects on performance. Above anaerobic threshold level, blood lactic acid level begins to rise sharply (see Figure 3.3, p. 55) For a recreational athlete this will occur at between 60 and 70 per cent of maximal oxygen uptake (75–80% MHR). An endurance-trained athlete can exercise at around 80–85% of VO_2max before lactic acid begins to accumulate rapidly. The two main reasons for this are:

- Endurance-trained athletes rely more on fat metabolism and lactic acid is not produced when fat breaks down.
- Endurance-trained athletes possess a greater density of mitochondrial reticulum, which allows more oxygen to be available to produce aerobic energy rather than forming lactic acid in the muscle fibres.

As will be seen in Chapter 3, the objective of endurance training is to elevate both VO₂max and anaerobic threshold as a percentage of that VO₂max. Chapter 3 will also discuss ways to establish anaerobic threshold using both laboratory and field testing.

A sound knowledge of the factors discussed in this chapter is important as the basis not only for understanding the rest of this book, but for developing training programs for speed and endurance athletes as well as team players.

More in-depth reading in the area of exercise physiology is suggested in the recommended reading list at the end of this chapter.

SUMMARY

- Energy for muscular work is obtained from the breakdown of ATP (adenosine triphosphate) in a reversible reaction, to form ADP (adenosine diphosphate) and P (phosphate). In order to resynthesise ATP, three energy systems (Creatine Phosphate, anaerobic glycolysis or lactic system, and aerobic or oxygen system) are used.
- The Creatine Phosphate system is used during maximal exercise of 10–20 seconds duration and takes up to five minutes to regenerate, which is why sprinters need long recoveries.
- Anaerobic glycolysis breaks down muscle stores of carbohydrate (glycogen) in the absence of oxygen to produce lactic acid and is particularly important during sprints longer than a few seconds. Lactic

acid is a major cause of fatigue and is removed more effectively from muscles and blood by light exercise during recovery.

- The aerobic or oxygen system burns fat, carbohydrate and protein in the presence of oxygen in order to provide energy for the remaking of ATP. This system is crucial for endurance athletes and for team players who need to recover quickly between bouts of high intensity exercise during a game.

- Skeletal muscle is made up of three different fibre types: type I (slow twitch), type IIa (fast oxidative) and type IIb (fast twitch).

- Different fibre types have different properties which make them more oxidative (endurance) or anaerobic (sprint). With increasing exercise intensity, these muscle fibres are recuited in the order: type I > type IIa > type IIb. Speed work or interval training will therefore recruit and train the type II fibres while slow endurance training will recruit the type I fibres.

- Maximal aerobic capacity (VO_2max) is the maximal amount of oxygen that can be transportd to, and consumed by, the working muscles during exercise. It is a product of three factors: maximal heart rate, maximal stroke volume (amount of blood pumped per beat) and maximal arterio-venous oxygen difference (the amount of oxygen extracted from the blood by the muscles).

- While VO_2max is important for endurance performance, the *percentage* of VO_2max that an athlete can exercise at for an extended period without accumulating lactic acid (anaerobic threshold) is more important.

RECOMMENDED READING

Baechle, T.R. (ed.) (1994) *Essentials of strength training and conditioning*, Human Kinetics, Champaign, Illinois.

Leger, L. & Boucher, R. (1980) 'An indirect continuous running multistage field test: The Université de Montreal track test', *Canadian Journal of Applied Sports Sciences*, 5, 77–84.

McArdle, W.D., Katch, F.I., & Katch, V.L. (1991) *Exercise Physiology: Energy, Nutrition and Human Performance*, Lea & Febiger, Philadelphia.

2

Training for speed

Lachlan Penfold and Dr David Jenkins

Careful analysis of an athlete's speed requirements must be the basis of any speed development program. Without understanding the specific nature of a sprinter or team player's game-requirements, sprint training is likely to be less than optimal; analysis of each activity is therefore essential. Such analysis makes it possible to train up to six different components which will each improve an athlete's sprint ability. Each component is briefly reviewed, along with 'sports speed', the speed required by a games-player rather than a track athlete. Recovery between sprints and sprint training sessions is discussed and the importance of both strength and plyometric training in speed development explained. The last two sections summarise the physiological responses to sprint exercise and explain the adaptations a player can expect from a successful sprint training program.

SPEED DEFINED

Speed has been defined as the ability to move the body or body parts through the required range of motion in the fastest time. Speed comprises reaction time, acceleration, maximum speed and speed endurance. It can also be considered as two separate components: the speed of a single movement (motor speed), and the capacity to move at the highest possible velocities (considered separately as acceleration and locomotor velocity). Acceleration and loco-motor velocity are decisive for all sprint events and are essential for performance in the majority of sport games (Harre, 1982).

Speed training must help the athlete to reach his/her maximum speed potential required for a particular sport and apply that speed to the specific sporting environment. For example, the person with the fastest straight line speed will not necessarily be the fastest player in game situations. Many sports require the athlete to stop, start, change direction, to move laterally and to travel backwards. Therefore, those athletes who suffer the least reduction in speed between their required sporting movements and their maximal speed, have the greatest chance to perform well.

ANALYSING SPEED REQUIREMENTS

Before developing a sprint training program, the speed qualities for both the sport and the athlete must be evaluated. In considering the sport, a coach or athlete must first decide whether speed is an important requirement. If so, it must be developed through all phases of training. What form of speed is required? Short intervals or long efforts? Is maximal speed reached, and if so, how often? Is speed endurance important? What are the movement patterns of the required speed (e.g. lateral, backwards, straight)?

From such an analysis it is possible to design training drills to accommodate the different speed requirements. It is important to remember that even within a team, different playing positions will often have different speed require-ments. Questions such as: 'Are there footwork requirements or body positions which change according to position?' and 'Can a player adapt his/her speed to the position or sport?' need to be asked.

The athlete's strengths and weaknesses must also be carefully evaluated before a speed program is put in place. Without analysis, the training program will be inadequate and the desired improvements will simply not occur.

Six areas to train

Following analysis of an athlete's sprint ability, attention must be directed at improving one or more specific areas of weakness. For the purposes of both analysis and training, sprint ability can be divided into six phases (Dick, 1989).

1. **Reaction to a signal** This is the ability to react to a signal or stimulus and can be improved with *reaction drills* (e.g. auditory, visual) and *starting drills.*
2. **Capacity to accelerate** This is the ability to reach maximal speed in the shortest possible time. It can be improved using the following:
   Acceleration drills (e.g. varied starting positions over 10–20m)(see Table 2.1, p. 32)
   Jumping training (e.g. plyometric activities such as depth jumps, standing longjumps, bounding)
   Strength training (e.g. squats, jump squats, power cleans and other power-related exercises)
3. **Capacity to readjust balance** This is the ability to prepare to execute one technique following the execution of an earlier technique and can be trained using:
   Proprioceptive drills (e.g. jumping/balance/stability drills)
   Lateral movement drills (e.g. shuttle runs)
   Deceleration techniques (e.g. stopping within a certain distance)
4. **Achievement of maximum speed** and
5. **Capacity to maintain maximum speed** These can be improved using:
   Absolute speed runs (e.g. 'flying' 30m sprints)
   Innervation drills (e.g. running at 100% all-out pace then, on instruction, putting in four fast steps)
   Overspeed runs (e.g. being towed behind a vehicle, being pulled by an elastic strap or sprinting downhill)

6. **Capacity to limit endurance factors on speed** This
   capacity can be trained by concentrating on:
   Speed endurance (e.g. repeated sprints with short recovery periods in between)
   Strength endurance (e.g. high repetition (15–50 reps)
   exercises in the gym)
   Specific work capacity development (e.g. sprints which
   mimic match conditions in terms of recovery)

Thus, if a player can sustain top speed for an acceptable
distance, but is lacking the ability to accelerate (and provided
acceleration is important to his/her performance), then training needs to concentrate on acceleration drills. On the other
hand, a player might be very quick off the mark but lack
the ability to maintain top speed. Again, provided maintenance of maximal speed is important for that athlete's sport
or playing position, training should address this relative
weakness. Needless to say, training should not concentrate
on aspects of fitness which are not important for performance.

It is possible to get an indication of sprint ability by
timing a player over a 120m sprint. If timing lights (or an
accurate time-keeper) can give the player's sprint time at
20m, 40m, 80m and 120m, a suitable training program can
be devised to address relative weakness in acceleration
(0–20m), maximal speed (40–80m) or speed endurance
(80–120m).

SPORTS SPEED

Sports speed can be defined as the speed required for a
particular game (either individual or team). It often involves
repeated efforts over a specified period of time and distance.

The major components of training sports speed include
linear/straight speed; lateral speed and agility (i.e. the ability
to move quickly in sideways directions; repeated speed
(i.e. the ability to repeat sprint efforts with only short periods
of time separating each bout); and speed while fatigued

(i.e. the ability to reproduce close to maximum speed throughout the duration of competition).

Linear/straight speed and lateral speed and agility can be further divided into acceleration, open field running and terminal speed:

Acceleration is a critical component of virtually all speed requirements for a team or individual player. Most players will only ever sprint over a distance of 1–30m, or 0.5–5 sec. While it is possible that a player will cover distances longer than 30m, the maximal speed component will normally not exceed this distance. Acceleration therefore has a most significant influence upon success in most sports. A player who is 1m quicker than his/her opponent over, for example, 15m, is able to break through a defensive gap (football), get around an opponent (basketball), get to the ball before it bounces twice (tennis/squash) and reach the base instead of being thrown out (baseball/softball). Acceleration must therefore form the foundation of any speed training program. When considering acceleration, *first step quickness* and *correct posture* are important.

First step quickness is the ability to move the body in the desired direction as quickly as possible. Often, speed improvements of 0.5–1.5m over 10m can be made by eliminating a false step. The false step is commonly seen when an athlete, wishing to run to the right, either rocks back onto the left leg or, even worse, takes a step back with the left leg, before beginning to run to the right. By teaching the athlete to drive straight forward in the intended direction, with a low, fast first step, time-wasting movements are avoided. As different open field sports require varying start positions, it is essential that most athletes can start sprinting from either foot.

Correct posture refers to the body position required for acceleration. It is vastly different to the posture necessary for maintaining maximal speed running. While maximal speed running requires a fairly upright torso (which allows the legs full range of movement through the pelvis), the optimal acceleration posture is between 45° and 60° (see Figure 2.1).

Figure 2.1: The correct and incorrect body positions for accelerating

If the athlete is stationary (as in, for example, baseball and softball) he/she should be able to get close to 45°. If the athlete is moving, less inertia must be overcome and therefore there is less need for such a low position. However, some degree of body angle is always needed for accelerating.

Open field running is common in sports where an athlete has room to move. It often involves a player running first at a submaximal pace and then accelerating to maximum speed for a required period of time or distance. Often this distance will be between 5m and 40m or 0.5sec and 6sec. It may also involve a change in direction, physical contact in pushing, being pushed, or breaking a tackle, carrying a ball, stick or racquet and being aware of the movements of opposition players and team mates. In this form of running, the ability to vary speed is important and a player who may have exceptional maximal speed may not seem particularly fast on the playing field if he/she is unable to adjust to these complications. Other factors important in this form of speed are the ability to correctly position the body for acceleration, and the ability to initiate a fast leg turnover. One drill which can train this is called the 'in/out' drill, in which the athlete increases speed over, for example, 15m, then sprints maximally for a distance of 20m, then slows down over a similar distance before reaccelerating and sprinting for a further 20m. It is also possible to incorporate changes in direction for lateral speed conditioning.

Terminal speed (or maximal speed) is normally reached between 40m and 60m in a 100m sprint but can only be maintained for a limited distance before deceleration sets in. The higher the level of anaerobic capacity or lactate tolerance, the longer the athlete can sustain maximal/terminal speed. For most games-players, maximal/terminal speed will rarely be a determining factor in their performance. For athletes such as track sprinters, however, speed over 100m and 200m is all important. Training will need to be specific to the demands of these individuals.

Many players still perform speed training at distances as long as 60m and rarely train at shorter distances. This emerges as non-specific when one considers the distances most players are expected to sprint. Of much greater value to many players would be a run over 80m comprising a 20m sprint (acceleration), 30m cruise (open field running), and a 30m sprint (re-acceleration). This allows the qualities of both acceleration and open field running to be trained to a much higher degree. Game-specific movement patterns and/or directional changes can be used to increase the specificity of the speed drill and ensure a good transfer of speed from training to playing.

Speed while fatigued

A number of team and individual sports are played over an extended period of time (e.g. football, tennis, baseball). Continued and varied physical demands during a match will require players to concentrate on factors other than just speed during competition. An athlete's level of fitness in areas such as speed and endurance will determine his/her ability to maintain sprint ability during a match. It must be emphasised that fitness is specific to each sport. For example, tennis and baseball are both played over an extended time period (2–4 hours) and involve short sprints both in a straight line and laterally. Both also require agility and the rotational movements of hitting and throwing. However, tennis players cover far more distance at low-to-medium exercise intensities, and have a significantly greater amount of rotational movements. Aerobic fitness is therefore important for tennis players to avoid an early onset of general fatigue as competition progresses. In contrast, the need for aerobic conditioning for baseball players is negligible. For most of the game, baseball players perform either at maximal intensity, or barely above rest. Thus, fitness for these players would best be improved by increasing the load of maximal intensity work (i.e., sprinting) rather than the volume of submaximal exercise (i.e. endurance training).

Time-motion analysis of a particular sport should determine the percentage of time an athlete performs exercise of differing intensities (e.g. jogging *vs* 80% maximal speed *vs* top speed). In addition, the frequency and duration of these movements can be recorded. Training can then be made more specific to the demands of the sport. As an example, speed training sessions are shown in Tables 2.1, 2.2 and 2.3, p. 32.

Recovery between sprints (within a session)

Recovery between sprints is a critical factor which can be altered depending on whether an athlete wants to develop maximal speed (in, for example, a one-off, all-out sprint) or anaerobic capacity (the ability to maintain multiple sprint performance). The key consideration in developing and improving maximal speed is for the muscles to have near-full reserves of creatine phosphate (CrP). At the start of a one-off sprint, creatine phosphate levels within a muscle are likely to be close to maximum. However, following even a brief sprint, it may take at least five minutes for creatine phosphate to be resynthesised. So if an athlete is forced during training to repeat a sprint before creatine phosphate has had sufficient time to resynthesise, that sprint will be slower, which is not desirable if the player wants to improve maximal speed.

Sometimes anaerobic capacity or lactate tolerance is trained, particularly when the games-player wants to mimic match conditions. In this type of training, the recovery between sprint bouts is deliberately kept short in order to progressively reduce the levels (and thus the contribution) of creatine phosphate in helping the muscles contract. This

Table 2.1: An example training session for improving acceleration

1. Warm-up and stretching

2. Plyometrics
     3 standing long jumps—two sets
     3 standing triple jumps—two sets
     4 standing medicine-ball throws—two sets
    30 seconds recovery between repetitions
    1–2 minutes recovery between sets

3. 5 × 10m sprints—three sets
    30–60 seconds recovery between repetitions
    2–4 minutes recovery between sets

4. 3 × 20m sprints (fall-forward start)—three sets
    60 seconds recovery between repetitions
    3–4 minutes recovery between sets

5. 2 × 30m sprints (start from lying on stomach)—two sets
    60 seconds recovery between repetitions
    3–4 minutes recovery between sets

6. Warm-down and stretching

Table 2.2: An example training session for improving maximal speed

1. Warm-up and stretching

2. Plyometrics
    Bounds—three sets of 10 repetitions
    Hop/Step—three sets of 5 reps. each leg
    2–3 minutes recovery between each set

3. 'Flying' 30m sprints (20m jog before the 30m sprint)—two sets of 3
       repetitions
    2–3 minutes recovery between repetitions
    5 minutes recovery between sets

4. 'Open-field' drill
    15m increasing speed—20m sprint—25m cruise—20m sprint—Two sets of
       three repetitions
    3–5 minutes recovery between repetitions
    5–8 minutes recovery between sets

5. 3 × 60m sprints
    6–8 minutes recovery between repetitions

6. Warm-down and stretching

Table 2.3: An example training session for improving anaerobic capacity

1. Warm-up and stretching

2. 10 × 10m sprints
     4 × 25m sprints
     3 × 50m sprints
     2 × 75m sprints
     1 × 100m sprint
     1 × 400m sprint
    All 100% effort
    recovery = walk back to the starting line

3. Warm-down and stretching

Note: *These drills are for 'straight-ahead' speed development only. Variations in stance and direction can be introduced for the training of lateral speed.*

puts an ever greater responsibility on anaerobic glycolysis (i.e. the lactic acid system) in meeting the exercise task and this in turn leads to a significant accumulation of lactic acid (and accelerated fatigue). The purpose of this type of training is to deliberately induce fatigue to cause the muscles to adapt to game-like situations.

A golden rule when maximal speed is being trained, is that a full recovery (often perhaps up to and even longer than five minutes) is necessary between sprints. An active low intensity recovery using an exercise such as jogging is known to be more effective than a passive recovery such as sitting or standing. For improving anaerobic capacity or lactate tolerance, keep the recovery periods brief to experience fatigue.

Recovery between sprint sessions

As stated above, for maximal speed to be improved, the athlete needs to be rested and fresh. Careful periodisation within each microcycle (i.e. a 7–10 day block) will help protect muscles from unwanted fatigue during sprint sessions and promote maximum improvements in speed. As explained in Chapter 5, the athlete cannot expect improvements in fitness from 'overtraining'; more is not always better.

Following a hard sprint session, the lactic acid in blood and muscle will disperse and return to normal levels within 30–45 minutes. Moreover, muscle glycogen (carbohydrate) stores can be replenished within 24 hours provided a high carbohydrate diet is consumed after training. However, despite near full recovery of fuel reserves within 24 hours, sprint training on consecutive days will prove counterproductive for most athletes. It is likely that after each hard training session, microscopic damage to the muscle fibres has occurred and that 24 hours is simply not long enough for repairs to take place. There is also something coaches refer to as 'central nervous system fatigue'. Although very little scientific evidence is available on this phenomenon, it seems likely that the nervous system (which is responsible for controlling maximal efforts during sprint exercise) may need an extended time to recover from an intense sprint session. Further research in this area is currently being conducted. However, athletes should normally avoid more than three well-spaced sprint training sessions each week.

PLYOMETRICS

Plyometrics are exercises which develop the explosive nature (i.e. power) of the muscles. Clearly, sprinting requires a high degree of power. If used properly, plyometrics can improve the speed at which the athlete exerts force. Before implementing any training program, it is important to analyse the movement requirements of the sport and, for plyometric training, the forms of power required for the event. The following questions need to be asked:

- What is the direction of force application?
- Is the major force exerted horizontally or vertically?
- Does the sport require lateral movement?
- How much time is available for force production?
- Is force production related to the speed of movement (which therefore involves decreased ground contact time), or to strength/force of movement (therefore being related to increased ground contact time and increased force production)?

Both the direction of force and time available for force production are important in deciding the type of plyometric exercises that should be incorporated into the training program. General plyometric exercises can be modified so as to be more specific to the required sporting movements. Many of the exercises beneficial for improved acceleration consist of short-response, shock-type movements such as bounding, jumping and skipping. The athlete should not perform these before being adequately prepared (i.e. having adequate strength and the correct technique); rather, plyometric exercises should be incorporated through the systematic progression of training loadings and follow the development of strength.

Plyometric training can either be integrated into both speed and strength training, or used as a separate training session. The relative complexity of the training session, in terms of both exercise selection and difficulty, will depend on the 'training age' of the athlete. This refers to the number of years an athlete has been training. For example, an 18 year old who has been training for three years will have a higher training age than a 20 year old who has only been training for two years. Given that technique is a critical component in many training methods, an advanced training age can allow athletes to progress to more demanding drills, irrespective of their chronological age. In general, plyometric training may be used before a strength training session, in conjunction with a speed or strength training session, or after a speed training session. Plyometric training should not be performed while tired or recovering from several days of very demanding training or playing.

The relative volume and intensity of both the plyometric session and any other session must be monitored closely so as to avoid any undue fatigue and excessive overload stress. Generally, if the intensity of each session is high, the volume must be low. The component which has been identified as the most important to train (e.g. speed, strength, endurance, power) will generally have the highest volume and be performed first. Less important training components must not interfere with the main aim of the training session. The density of training must also be closely monitored. Density refers to the amount of each training component per training session or groups of sessions. Generally, the higher the intensity of the training component, the lower the density.

One further consideration must be the plyometric component of the sport. In sports that have a high plyometric demand (e.g. volleyball, basketball) the density of plyometric training should be carefully monitored. Generally these sports have a lower training density due to the high plyometric demands incurred from actually playing the sport. Remember, plyometric training must not be undertaken while fatigued.

STRENGTH TRAINING

Many athletes will require varying degrees of strength for the different demands placed on them in competition. Methods to improve maximal strength, power and strength endurance may all need to be incorporated into an athlete's training program at some stage. Although it is beyond the purpose of this text to detail specific strength training programs, it must be stressed that sprinters should develop a high level of structural strength which allows the athlete to maintain the correct body posture required for speed training. The strength of abdominal, hip and lower back muscles must therefore be a central element in a strength training program. This is also referred to as core strength, and is needed to maintain the correct body position for all phases of sprinting, from acceleration through to maximum speed.

When a person accelerates, strength is required to overcome the inertia of body mass. Thus, a sport requiring frequent bursts of acceleration (e.g. baseball, softball) requires high levels of maximum strength. Once maximal strength has been improved, the athlete can move on to more explosive exercises (e.g. power cleans, jump squats) that develop power.

PHYSIOLOGICAL RESPONSES TO SPRINT EXERCISE

Although the precise cause/s of fatigue during sprint exercise is/are still unknown to us, scientists have identified a number of mechanisms which may possibly be responsible for the failure to maintain peak power output for more than a few seconds.

It is clear that the problems of fatigue are related to the muscles being used for the sprint. Our understanding of these so called 'intramuscular events' has improved enormously since the reintroduction of the needle biopsy technique in the mid-1960s. This procedure involves the extraction of small pieces of muscle tissue under local anaesthetic. By comparing changes in the chemistry of muscle sampled before and immediately after a sprint, a number of major changes which could adversely affect performance have been identified. These include:

1. The muscle becomes significantly acidic (due to extensive reliance on anaerobic glycolysis, which leads to lactic acid production). Given that the functions of a number of enzymes and muscle contraction are impaired by acidosis, scientists and coaches alike have long considered that an excess production of lactic acid is a principal cause of fatigue during sprint exercise. Debate continues as to which mechanism in the muscle is more seriously affected by the acidosis, the energy pathways (i.e. the enzymes which produce energy) or the contractile proteins (which produce the force).

2. A significant decrease in creatine phosphate concentrations. This is certainly related to the initial fall in peak power output which typically occurs soon after the start of a sprint.

3. Excessive loss of potassium ions (K^+) from the contracting muscles to the blood as a result of the rapid series of maximal contractions needed to perform a sprint. This has been attributed to the failure of small 'pumps' which normally manage to keep the K^+ in the muscle. During high intensity exercise such as sprinting or weight training, K^+ is lost from the muscles with each contraction and quite simply, the capacity of these pumps is surpassed. When K^+ is lost from a tissue, the ability to transmit electrical signals from the central nervous system to the muscles is impaired. This can result in fatigue.

4. Reduction in calcium release within the muscle cell wall during exercise. Calcium is needed for the muscle fibres to contract.

At the present time, we can only conclude that all these events probably contribute in some way or another to fatigue during high intensity exercise. Only further research will allow us to identify the most important mechanism/s in the fatigue process. Much of the research into this area is motivated by a desire to tailor appropriate training programs to the specific needs of sprinters. Given that the cause of a sprinter's fatigue is clearly in the muscle, only careful examination of muscle tissue pre- and post-exercise will provide the necessary answers.

ADAPTATIONS TO SPRINT TRAINING

Improvements in performance as a result of a period of sprint training have been attributed to one or more of several changes:

1. An athlete will often increase his/her leg strength in response to the increased impact forces imposed by a sprint training program. Improved leg strength will in turn assist power output and improve sprint performance.
2. The trained motor units (i.e. nerves and muscle fibres) fire with greater synchronisation after sprint training. This improves the collective contribution which individual fibres make to sprint exercise. Consider the pre- and post-training difference to be similar to the performance of a car before and after a mechanical tuning; the result is improved efficiency.
3. The key enzyme in anaerobic glycolysis phosphofructo-kinase (PFK), increases its activity. This simply enhances the muscle's ability to provide energy through anaerobic glycolysis. However, one of the biochemical consequences of increased anaerobic glycolysis is increased production of lactic acid (which, as explained in the previous section, is still implicated in the fatigue process).
4. Improved mechanisms to cope with the increased acid load. There are two changes which are believed to accommodate this. First, within muscles, the buffering capacity increases. This is the muscle's ability to 'mop-up' the excess acid, at least for a few extra seconds of exercise (which is all the advantage that an elite sprinter seeks from a training program). Second, the muscle fibre improves its ability to move the lactic acid outside the cell and into the blood during exercise. This protects the

muscle fibres and enzymes and allows the athlete to delay the rate at which fatigue sets in.

5. The muscles improve their ability to retain potassium which facilitates continued transmission of electrical signals from the central nervous system. This maintains contraction and the high work output.

6. Control of calcium within the contracting muscle fibre improves with sprint training. This helps the muscle maintain the necessary relaxation–contraction cycling.

In considering any adaptation to training, it is important to think of improvements as helping the athlete to *delay* the onset of fatigue, not to avoid the fatigue process. In the case of the sprint athlete, most sprinters fatigue at some stage during their event. Thus, it is the *rate* of fatigue which training can influence, and the winner of a 400m sprint on the track is invariably the runner who fatigues the least.

In summary, the type of speed needed in a particular event, sport or game must first be carefully assessed. This is critical if the speed training program is to be both effective and specific. For games players, acceleration is likely to be the most important component of speed; first-step quickness and correct body posture are both central to ensuring good acceleration. Recovery between sprints is another very important consideration when devising a training program; when training to improve 'pure' speed, a long recovery will be necessary to allow full resynthesis of creatine phosphate. Alternatively, when training to improve anaerobic capacity, recovery periods between sprints can be kept relatively brief. Finally, any speed training program will benefit from both strength and plyometric training. These need to be carefully arranged into the overall training plan; Chapter 5 will address the concept of periodisation of speed training.

SUMMARY

- Before devising a speed training program, the type of speed an athlete requires must first be analysed. It is then possible to decide on the relative attention which acceleration, maximal speed and/or speed endurance should receive during training.
- Acceleration can be improved by ensuring that the athlete assumes a low (45°) body position at the start of a sprint and by eliminating any false movement which is not in the direction of the sprint.
- When training to improve maximal speed, recovery between sprints is very important. An inadequate recovery period will prevent the athlete from achieving top speed again (which is essential for speed to improve).
- When training to improve anaerobic capacity or lactate tolerance, the recovery periods between sprints should be kept brief. This causes an overload of lactic acid in the muscles which in turn promotes an improved ability to cope with acidosis.
- Strength and plyometric training will both help to improve sprint performance. However, athletes need to carefully plan such sessions so as to avoid undue fatigue. Strength training should also precede a general shift to plyometrics during a training period.

RECOMMENDED READING

Dick, F. (1989) *Sports Training Principles*, A & C Black, London.
Dintiman, G. and Ward, R. (1988) *Sport Speed*, Leisure Press, Champaign, Illinois.
Harre, D. (1982) *Principles of Sports Training*, Sportvelag, Berlin.
Newsholme, E., Leech, T. and Duester, G. (1994) *Keep on Running*, John Wiley and Sons, Chichester.
Radcliffe, J. and Farentinos, R. (1985) *Plyometrics*, Human Kinetics, Champaign, Illinois.

3

Training for endurance

Dr Peter Reaburn

Endurance is the ability to last. Whether it be to survive a marathon run, a 40-kilometre time trial on the bike, a six-minute rowing race or a 1500m swim, the athlete must have the ability to finish the event. Team players such as netballers or footballers must also have endurance, not only to last the game but to recover both from sprints in the game and from game to game if playing in a number of games in a day or on successive days. This chapter outlines the factors that affect endurance capacity, the factors related to successful endurance performance, and then gives practical advice on how to maximise endurance development.

FACTORS INFLUENCING ENDURANCE ABILITY

Five factors determine the ability to be a good endurance athlete. They are genetics, gender, body composition, age and training.

Genetics

It has been estimated through studies on identical twins that 70–75% of endurance ability is genetic. That is, our parents have given us (or have failed to give us!) the ability to be an endurance athlete. They have given us a particular body type, a possible endurance physiology, a high or low percentage of slow twitch endurance muscle fibres, the ability to recover from or adapt to training stress, and the mental constitution for endurance. If we don't have these factors in our favour, we are going to find it difficult to do well in endurance events.

Gender

Female endurance athletes *generally* have a 10% lower aerobic capacity than male endurance athletes. This is because females have smaller hearts which therefore pump less blood and oxygen, a smaller concentration of haemoglobin (the substance in the blood that carries oxygen), and carry greater amounts of body fat than men. While it might be argued that extra fat may lead to better flotation in female distance swimmers, it is generally agreed that the extra fat found in most females is a hindrance to their endurance performance when compared to males by increasing frontal resistance.

Body composition

Low levels of body fat are very important to the endurance athlete. No endurance athlete wants to carry extra weight around on a bike or on a running track, on a playing field or through the water.

Age

Age is a critical factor influencing aerobic capacity. Aerobic capacity declines in non-exercising older people at approximately 1% per year, and in veteran athletes at 0.5% per year. The major factor explaining this decline is a reduction in maximal heart rate at the rate of approximately one beat per year.

Training

Endurance training improves both the ability of the heart to pump blood to the muscles and the ability of those trained muscles to take up and use the oxygen made available by the heart and blood. Research suggests that training can increase aerobic capacity by up to 25%.

While there is little that can be done about genetics, gender and age, dieting and exercising safely can reduce body fat and endurance can be improved by using correct training methods. These training methods will be discussed shortly, but first an examination of the physiological factors that lead to successful endurance performance will be undertaken.

FACTORS RELATED TO SUCCESSFUL ENDURANCE PERFORMANCE

Sports science has conclusively shown that performance in endurance events or sports is due not only to the factors outlined above but to a number of specific physiological characteristics. These are discussed in detail below.

Maximal oxygen uptake (VO₂max) or aerobic capacity

VO_2max is the greatest rate at which oxygen can be consumed by an athlete. The units of VO_2max are ml/kg/min and the values of some outstanding athletes have been measured as: Said Aouita (5000m runner)—83.0; John Walker (miler)—82.0; Seb Coe (miler)—77.0; Greta Waitz (female marathon)—73.5; Peter Snell (miler)—72.3; Derek Clayton (marathon)—69.7. Values in young, elite male runners might be 65–75ml/kg/min but in male runners aged 60-plus they are around 50–55ml/kg/min, with females about 10% lower. Swimmers and cyclists usually have a lower aerobic capacity due to their smaller muscle mass which can therefore take up less oxygen (see Table 3.1).

Historically, it was thought (and still is by many coaches and athletes!) that VO_2max was the most critical factor in

Table 3.1: Typical values of maximal oxygen uptake in various sports

Type of event	Maximal oxygen uptake ($ml.kg^{-1}.min^{-1}$)	
	Men	Women
Endurance sports		
Long-distance running	75–80	65–70
Road cycling	70–75	60–65
Middle-distance running	70–75	65–68
Orienteering	65–72	60–65
Swimming	65–70	55–60
Rowing	65–69	60–64
Canoeing	60–68	50–55
Walking	60–65	55–60
Games		
Football (soccer)	50–57	–
Volleyball	55–60	48–52
Basketball	50–55	40–45
Tennis	48–52	40–45
Table tennis	40–45	38–42
Combative sports		
Boxing	60–65	–
Wrestling	60–65	–
Judo	55–60	48–52
Fencing	45–50	40–45
Power sports		
Sprint track and field (100m, 200m)	48–52	43–47
Long jump	50–55	45–50
Decathlon, heptathlon	60–65	50–55
Weightlifting	40–50	–
Discus throwing, shot-putting	40–45	35–40
Javelin throwing	45–50	42–47
Pole-vaulting	45–50	–
Technical–acrobatic sports		
Figure skating	50–55	45–50
Gymnastics	45–50	40–45
Rhythmic gymnastics	–	40–45
Shooting	40–45	35–40

endurance performance. Wrong! While it is important, it is not *the* most critical factor when it comes to performance on the track, road, lake, river or pool. While this capacity is important, a far better predictor of endurance performance is what fraction or percentage of that VO_2max can be maintained for the duration of an event—a concept called the anaerobic threshold.

Anaerobic threshold

This is the percentage of the athlete's aerobic capacity or VO_2max that can be used at race pace—the 'hurt but hold' intensity. Top marathoners and road cyclists can maintain 80–90% of their VO_2max while less elite athletes can only sustain 70–75% for the same distance. Above this pace the muscles start to produce lactic acid which upsets the muscle contraction process and slows the breakdown of carbohydrate so that energy production is compromised.

To highlight the importance of the anaerobic threshold to endurance performance we will look at one of the world's greatest former marathoners, Australian Derek Clayton. Derek held the world marathon record for over a decade during the 1960s and 1970s. Lab tests showed that his VO_2max was lower than most of his competitors. However, his anaerobic threshold was relatively higher than theirs, giving him an edge when it came to racing. History also tells us he was mentally tough—he passed blood in his urine and faeces for days after breaking the world record! Later we will discuss ways to measure the anaerobic threshold and ways to help raise it so that we can race harder and not accumulate lactic acid.

Fatigue resistance

This is the ability of an endurance athlete to maintain pace during prolonged endurance exercise. Fatigue resistance is a major adaptation to long duration, low intensity endurance training. The long slow distance and 'miles in the arms or legs' concept does allow an athlete to resist fatigue.

Economy of motion

This is the oxygen cost required to maintain a specific speed. Elite endurance athletes, through better technique, use up to 15% less oxygen to maintain a pace than recreational athletes. Technique is critical in improving economy, with runners ideally having a relaxed upper body; cyclists should not throw their upper body around but keep it relaxed; the extraneous 'actions' of tension use up valuable fuel and oxygen but don't produce speed. Longer, slower work in running, cycling, swimming and rowing improves economy.

Fuel usage

At high race speeds there is a greater reliance on carbohydrate than on fat as a fuel for energy production. Well-trained endurance athletes can, however, make greater use of fats as a fuel during racing than less-trained athletes, thereby conserving valuable liver and muscle carbohydrate (glycogen) stores.

Through the correct training techniques, we can adapt our bodies to maximise each of these above factors.

TRAINING TECHNIQUES FOR SUCCESSFUL ENDURANCE PERFORMANCE

It is common practice among many coaches and athletes to adopt the prevailing training methods used by current world class athletes in their sports. This approach has not only led to many a good athlete burning out but also has fostered the belief that more is better, with an emphasis on 'big mileage' being seen as the key to successful endurance performance.

In a recent study on young swimmers, well-respected USA sports scientist and masters athlete, David Costill, halved the volume of training being undertaken by a swim squad and found no change in swim performance compared to a squad which maintained twice the volume of work. This research strongly argues against the belief that more is better. Indeed, the training research currently available recommends a combination of quantity and quality as the key to endurance performance.

Endurance training intensities

Due to the relationship between training intensity (speed) and heart rate being a straight line (Figure 3.1), heart rates can be used as a means of determining training intensity.

The intensities are based on endurance athletes knowing their own maximal heart rates for their chosen sport(s). It is

47

Figure 3.1: The straight line relationships between exercise intensity and both heart rate and oxygen consumption. VO₂max is indicated by the relative plateau in oxygen consumption at the highest exercise intensity

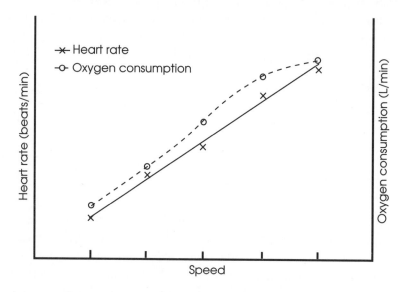

important to understand that maximal heart rate (and VO$_2$max), even within an individual athlete, is invariably different for swimming, cycling, running, rowing, etc. due to the different muscle masses being used and the different body positions involved in each sport.

While it is strongly recommended that maximal heart rates for an older (>40 years) athlete be determined at a sports science laboratory with a doctor in attendance, experienced and healthy endurance athletes may decide to determine maximal heart rate themselves. This can be done by warming up well, then doing 10 continuous one-minute increases in intensity, starting easy then gradually building till the last minute is flat out. The test should be done wearing a heart rate monitor and be followed by a 10–15 minute warm-down.

Once maximal heart rate has been determined, Table 3.2 can be used to establish heart rate training zones.

These heart rate zones are scientifically-based guidelines but they are *only guidelines*. Too many endurance athletes

Table 3.2: Endurance training zone guidelines: intensities based on percentages of maximal heart rate

Zone	Name	Intensity
1	Recovery	<65% Max HR
2	Aerobic	65–75% Max HR
3	Extensive endurance	75–80% Max HR
4	Intensive endurance	80–85% Max HR
5	Anaerobic threshold	85–90% Max HR
6	Maximal aerobic	>90% Max HR

become slaves to a heart rate monitor or to a heart rate that they saw in one of the many heart rate training books available. Many of these books assume each person has a maximum heart rate of 220 minus age, or that the level 2 training zone can be determined by taking your age from 180. The only real ways to determine your maximal heart rate are in a laboratory or by using the incremental test referred to above.

When using heart rate zones and a heart rate monitor, it is important to remember that heart rates will be higher when exercising in hot and/or humid conditions. This is due to the fact that an athlete training in the heat may dehydrate slightly through sweat loss. This lowers blood volume which results in the heart having to pump harder and more quickly to get the same amount of blood and oxygen to the working muscles. Secondly, when training in the heat, blood is diverted to the skin to help offload the heat generated in the muscles. Again, the heart has to work harder to keep the amount of blood pumping to the muscles to give them the oxygen they require to maintain speed.

Research suggests that heart rates during submaximal work increase by 1.4% for each degree above 21°C. For example, at a constant pace, a heart rate of 140 at 21°C will become 160 at 31°C.

Bearing these considerations in mind, let us now discuss each of the training zones summarised in Table 3.2 individually.

Zone 1 is the recovery zone and can be achieved using the sport the athlete is training for or by some other method such as water running or cross-training. The important factor here is that intensity is low and duration short. This type of 'training' is useful after racing, after hard training sessions such as those in levels 5 or 6, or when the body says it's time to lighten the load.

Zone 2 is the minimum intensity required to give an endurance training response. The beginner endurance athlete might start out at 65% of MHR; as fitness improves or the years accumulate, the intensity required to gain adaptations will increase. The adaptations that occur with this level of training include:

- increased stroke volume (amount of blood pumped per heartbeat)
- increased oxygen transport in the blood
- increased blood volume
- increased ability of the muscles to use oxygen
- increased capillary (blood vessel) density within the trained muscles
- improved mobilisation and use of fat as a fuel.

This type of training, together with level 3 extensive endurance training, forms the basis of endurance training and should be performed for a minimum of 30 minutes depending on the event being trained for. Obviously an Ironman (person!) triathlete would need to spend many more hours on level 2 training if they need to swim for 1–2 hours, ride for 5–8 hours, and then run a marathon. Endurance athletes should aim for a minimum frequency of three training sessions per week, with up to 10–12 sessions per week for the more competitive and experienced athlete. This level of training should be emphasised during the preparation phase of the training year or season and never forgotten during the other phases.

Zone 3 training is done at 75–80% of maximal heart rate for long periods (hence extensive endurance). Examples are 10–30km runs, 40–120km rides, 5–15km rows, or 1500–3000m swims, or longer sets of intervals. This type of training takes place during the preparation phase of training and induces similar adaptations to those noted above for level 2 training.

Zone 4 training is performed just below anaerobic threshold and because intensity is lifted, duration is reduced. Examples are 5–20km runs, 30–80km rides, 5–15km rows, or more intense intervals. Importantly, the intensity is just below 'hurt but hold' anaerobic threshold intensity and is thus 'strong but comfortable'. The adaptations that occur with this training include:

- elevation of VO_2max
- elevation of anaerobic threshold
- improvement in economy or efficiency.

Zone 5 It is difficult to understand how training at large volumes below planned race pace (zones 2 to 4) can possibly prepare you for racing (zones 5 and 6). It is therefore important to undertake some training at the anaerobic threshold (zone 5). This type of training aims to expose the body to sustained exercise corresponding to the endurance athlete's highest current steady state pace. The experienced athlete can determine the pace for these longer workouts or intervals by calculating current time trial pace minus 5% or by doing a 30-minute time trial at steady state (no sprint at the end) and observing the heart rate at the end of the time trial. In general, this intensity can be described as the 'hurt but hold' intensity. The adaptations that take place with this type of training are:

- elevation of VO_2max
- raising of the anaerobic threshold
- increased removal of lactic acid
- decreased production of lactic acid
- specific nervous system patterning of the muscle fibres needed during racing.

The intensity of training is elevated to 85–90% of maximal heart rate and can be done through continuous work of at least 20 minutes duration but no longer than 60–90 minutes (5–20km runs; 20–60km rides; 1500m swims). After this the muscles will run out of energy in the form of carbohydrate. Another form of zone 5 training is interval training with short recoveries that are half or less of the work time

Figure 3.2: An example of heart rates during work and rest intervals when performing anaerobic threshold interval training

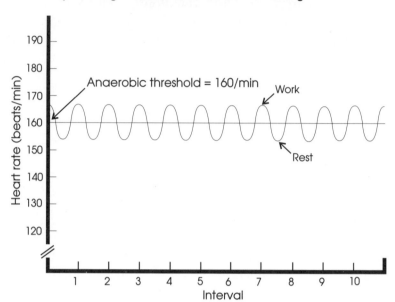

(10–15 × 100m swims; 15–20 × 1km cycles; 8–10 × 400m runs) (Figure 3.2).

It is important with anaerobic threshold training intervals that the quality of the last interval should be as good as the quality of the first interval and the recovery relatively short compared to the interval duration. This type of training should be performed at the most 2 or 3 times per week, should be preceded by a good warm-up, followed by a good warm-down, and generally be preceded and followed by an easier (zones 1 or 2) day.

During anaerobic threshold training periods, recovery after and between training sessions is critical and base training intensities (zones 1 to 2) should not be forgotten. Recovery can also be enhanced by eating or drinking carbohydrate-rich foods, since both zones 5 and 6 training mainly use muscle and liver carbohydrate as their energy source and supplies will be depleted after such training. The carbohydrates should have a high glycaemic index (see Chapter 8) and be consumed ideally within the first 30 minutes after training but critically within two hours after training.

Zone 6 or maximal aerobic training employs intervals with speeds that are greater than planned race pace but with long recoveries. The overall training volume is reduced but the intensity is lifted during this final pre-competition phase, which lasts 4 to 6 weeks. Again, recovery (zones 1 and 2) after these sessions is critical. Zones 2–5 training intensities should not be forgotten during this phase. Examples of this type of training are 3–8 minute repeats (300–400m swims; 5km reps on the bike; 1km reps on the run track) with 3–6 minute active recoveries (easy swim, spinning or jog). Intensity is 90–100% of maximal heart rate for each interval but recovery intensity is down to 60–70% of maximal heart rate. Athletes should be well warmed up and build into the first 30 seconds of each interval. Repetitions depend on individual tolerances but 4–10 reps are suggested depending on the individual athlete, their training age (years of training), fitness level, predisposition to injury, and whether the athlete swims, bikes or runs, which have an increasing 'tear-down' factor. At the most, two sessions of zone 6 per week should be used with easy recovery work in between. Adaptations that take place with this type of training include:

- increased tolerance to lactic acid
- elevated VO_2max
- improved endurance speed.

METHODS FOR DETERMINING ANAEROBIC THRESHOLD

As you may have gathered from the above discussion, anaerobic threshold training is critical for strong performances in endurance events. While determining this intensity can be done using 85–90% of maximal heart rate, athletes need to know their maximal heart rate. A triathlete will need to know his or her maximal heart rate for swim, bike and run; the rates are *usually* different with running generally the highest, cycling approximately 10 beats per minute lower,

Table 3.3:	Maximal and training heart rates of a 20-year-old male triathlete swimming, cycling and running		
	Swimming	**Cycling**	**Running**
Maximal heart rate (MHR)	185	190	200
Endurance zone 2 (65–75% MHR)	<139	<143	<150
Endurance zones 3–4			
Extensive endurance (75–80% MHR)	139–148	143–152	150–160
Intensive endurance (80–85% MHR)	148–157	152–162	160–170
Endurance zone 5 (85–92% MHR)	157–170	162–175	170–184
Endurance zone 6 (>92% MHR)	>170	>175	>184

Note: All numbers are heart rates measured in beats per minute (bpm)

and swimming the lowest at 10–20 beats lower than running (Table 3.3).

Other methods of measuring anaerobic threshold heart rates include the lactate curve, the Conconi test or a time trial.

Lactate curve

A lactate curve is usually done in a sports science laboratory under the supervision of an exercise physiologist. It involves working progressively harder (running faster, pushing bigger gears, increasing time per 500m on a rowing ergometer) every 3–5 minutes while blood is taken and heart rates recorded. Lactate is produced in relatively large amounts when the muscles begin working anaerobically (in the absence of enough oxygen). Once produced in the muscles, the lactate moves into the blood where it is removed via the heart, the liver and other muscles. When the concentration of lactate in the blood rises dramatically, scientists have suggested the athlete is at anaerobic threshold (Figure 3.3).

Because we know the speed, gearing or time per 500m at which lactate began to rise, we can determine the heart rate at which anaerobic threshold occurred. While it is the most valid method for threshold determination, it generally requires sports scientists and quite expensive equipment to measure it.

Conconi method

The Conconi method for anaerobic threshold determination

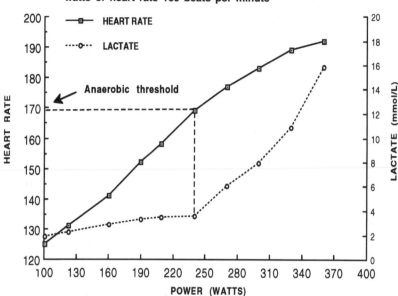

Figure 3.3: Blood lactate responses of a rower to increased exercise intensity (watts) on a rowing machine. Note the rise in blood lactate at 240 watts or heart rate 169 beats per minute

was developed by an Italian sports scientist named Conconi who worked with former world one-hour cycling champion Francesco Moser. The principle of this test is that the work rate (speed, power) is increased every 30–60 seconds and the heart rate recorded at the end of each period using a heart rate monitor. You then plot a graph of speed against heart rate (Figure 3.4).

Conconi believes that heart rate increases in a straight line until a particular speed (anaerobic threshold) is reached, at which the heart rate line curves downwards. Australian experience with this method is that it works with some athletes but not with most. However, the beauty of the test is its simplicity; the only equipment needed is a heart rate monitor and a pen and paper. Contact the suppliers of Polar Heart Rate Monitors for more details on the Conconi test.

Time trial

Time trials should be done over at least 30 minutes on an

Figure 3.4: **Diagram of the velocity of heart rate deflection (V$_d$) and associated anaerobic threshold heart rate as determined using the Conconi method**

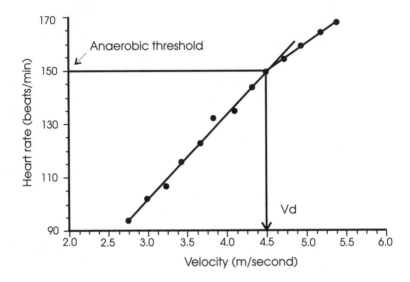

uninterrupted course (pool early on a Saturday, windtrainer, rowing ergometer, or run track) and at a steady state pace with no sprint at the end. The aim is to self-select a pace the athlete can maintain continuously for the time trial with no sprints or change in pace. The heart rate at the end will be very close to the athlete's anaerobic threshold. Again, the beauty of this test is its simplicity. However, experience suggests that this test is most useful for experienced athletes who know how to hold pace well.

PERIODISATION OF ENDURANCE TRAINING

Having examined the different endurance training intensities, athletes and coaches need to make decisions on how to put these training intensities together—leading to the concept of periodisation.

The art of training correctly is to put the various training intensities together during a week (microcycle) or 3–4 week block (macrocycle) to maximise training time and prevent overtraining. Hard, medium and easy days, weeks or three to four-week blocks are manipulated to stress the body at times and then to allow the body to adapt to that stress. While Chapter 5 of this book discusses the concept of periodisation in detail, here we will give some specific examples on how one might periodise the training periods for endurance athletes.

A microcycle of a week might consist of six training sessions with a day off but with two periods of easy, medium, hard days. During the base development or preparation phase when the athlete is getting the 'miles in the legs' or 'kms into the arms', the terms easy, medium and hard might refer to distances covered getting longer or to intensity zones 2–4 being manipulated while distances are held constant. During the specific preparation or mid-season phase, the same easy, medium, hard schedule might be in place, but hard might be zone 6, medium zone 4, and easy zone 2.

A macrocycle for endurance might be a 3–4 week period where a hard week is followed by an easy week, then a medium week. Again assuming six sessions a week, a hard week mid-season might be 2 × zones 2 or 3, 1 × zone 4, 1 × zone 5, and 1 × zone 6, with an easy week being 1 × zone 6, 1 × zone 1, 3 × zone 2, 1 × zone 5. The athlete must remember the objective of each phase but, as a rule of thumb, increase volume through early season phase, lift intensity and drop volume during mid-season, and do the same during the competition phase.

The endurance training year or season can be broken up into four main phases: base or foundation; transition; speed/power training and taper.

Base or foundation training is performed during the non-competitive period of the training year and builds the aerobic base on which more intense training is built. Zones 2–4 are emphasised with kilometres gradually built up. This phase may last up to 12 or 16 weeks, depending on the time lag between the athlete's last competitive phase and his or her experience.

Transition training or mid-season training can last 6–8 weeks and is done by introducing zones 4–5. Recovery between zone 5 sessions is important to allow quality work to be done during those sessions. Volume (km) drops but intensity is lifted during this phase. Any races entered during this phase should be considered zone 5 training.

Speed and power training is undertaken in the last 4–6 weeks where, although all other levels are maintained, level 6 work is introduced to give endurance speed. Volumes are reduced as a result of the intensity being high.

Injuries may occur during the transition and speed/power phases because intensities are so high. 'Listening' to the body during these phases is essential and recovery methods (see Chapter 6) should be used extensively. Importantly, both threshold and maximal aerobic power training are difficult and should only be undertaken by healthy athletes who have no cardiac risk factors, a training age of 2–3 years, are not prone to overuse injuries, and who have undertaken an extensive foundation phase. As a general rule, when doing quality work (zones 5–6), be fresh; quality counts!

Tapering or peaking is a highly individual matter but usually takes place during the last 7–10 days prior to major competition and involves a gradual or dramatic reduction in training volume (km). Both training frequency and intensity should be maintained. A recent study found that middle distance runners significantly improved their performance by sharply reducing their training *volume* while maintaining or increasing their training *intensity* seven days before a race. This taper method was superior to both a reduction in training intensity and total rest in the week prior to competition. It is generally accepted that the longer the athlete has been training, the longer the taper can be. However, if training duration has been short, a 'drop dead' taper of 2–3 days where volume is dropped dramatically might be recommended.

A correctly planned endurance training program, that emphasises a strong base followed by 'hits' of higher quality anaerobic threshold and maximal aerobic intervals, will allow the endurance athlete to optimise her/his genetic potential. Because endurance training involves long and sometimes intense training, the training program needs to be periodised to allow for adequate recovery times both within a week and from week to week.

While the principles of training such as specificity, progressive overload and recovery are important, the smart endurance athlete must obey the most important training principle of all—listen to the body!

SUMMARY

- Five factors determine the ability to be a good endurance athlete—genetics, gender, body composition, age and training. Training will improve endurance performance by developing maximal oxygen uptake (VO_2max), anaerobic threshold, resistance to fatigue, economy, and fuel usage.
- Endurance can be developed by training at a number of differing heart rate intensities based on percentages of maximal heart rate. Each of these training intensities will stimulate specific adaptations that improve endurance performance.
- Maximal heart rate is dependent upon age, muscle mass used in the sport, and the body position. Healthy athletes should establish their maximal heart rates for each sport they are training for.
- Anaerobic threshold heart rates can be determined using percentage of maximal heart rate (85–90%), a lactate curve, the Conconi method, or a time trial over 30–40 minutes.
- In general, endurance should be periodised so that an athlete gradually adapts to both higher training distances and/or intensity. It is crucial that an athlete is allowed time to adapt to quality endurance training.

- Tapering or peaking for endurance involves dropping training volume (kms) while maintaining both training frequency and intensity.

RECOMMENDED READING

Borysewicz, E. (1989) *Bicycle Road Racing*, Vitesse Press, Brattleboro, Vermont.
Burke, L. (1992) *The Complete Guide to Food for Sports Performance*, Allen & Unwin, Sydney; rev. edn. 1995.
Burke, L. & Deakin, V. (eds) (1994) *Clinical Sports Nutrition*, McGraw-Hill, Sydney.
Cedaro, R. (1992) *Triathlon: Into the Nineties*, Murray Child & Co., Sydney.
Killmier, A. (ed.) (1992) *Mastering Swimming: A Self-help Guide for Coaches and Swimmers*, Fraser Publications, Melbourne.
Maglischo, E.W. (1993) *Swimming Even Faster*, Mayfield, Mountain View, USA.
Martin, D.E. & Coe, P.N. (1991) *Training Distance Runners*, Human Kinetics, Champaign, Illinois.
Newsholme, E., Leech, T., & Duester, G. (1994) *Keep on Running: The Science of Training and Performance*, Wiley & Sons, London.
Tinley, S. & McAlpine, K. (1994) *Scott Tinley's Winning Guide to Sports Endurance: How to Maximize Speed, Strength and Stamina*, Kangaroo Press, Sydney.

4

Speed and endurance training for team games players

Craig Maskiell

Many of the principles used in developing a training program for any athlete are relevant to the games player, but allowances must be made for the differences brought about by direct competition with opposition players, the importance of the skills required and the importance of addressing a team as a group. The areas that coaches and athletes must consider include determining the event requirements, fitness testing, goal establishment, and program development and implementation for the pre-season and the competitive season.

Determining the event requirements

Knowledge of the physical requirements of a sport is essential for the development of training programs for games players. In addition, programs must be individualised to accommodate the considerable differences which can exist between different playing positions. To allow the development of an effective training program which specifically applies to particular positional responsibilities, a coach and/or athlete must first carefully assess what precisely is required of a particular playing position. The two approaches most commonly used are time-motion analysis and heart rate analysis.

Time-motion analysis normally involves videotaping the athlete during competition. Careful scrutiny of the footage then allows a number of activities to be quantified. These may include: total distance covered; total distance sprinted, jogged and walked; length of time in average sprint effort; length of time between sprint efforts; time spent in direct physical contact and time spent standing still.

Time spent sprinting, jogging and being involved in physical contact may be considered active periods, while walking and standing still may be considered recovery periods. Work-rest ratios can be calculated on the relationship between these two categories and a training program developed to mimic these demands. Given that a player's activity level is likely to change considerably during the course of a game, time-motion analysis should ideally assess the *entire* game or event.

Heart rate (HR) can be used either independently of time-motion analysis or to supplement the video analysis. It can provide an indication of relative effort on the cardiovascular system and is particularly useful in setting the intensities of running drills during training. However, collecting heart rate data during competition may not be easy, especially in contact sports.

Fitness testing

Regular fitness testing provides an assessment of a player's overall ability. It also identifies potential problems with a player's physical abilities and allows training programs to be developed to concentrate on particular aspects of fitness. Typically, a team's training season will follow a general transition from general conditioning through to specific, game-type activities as the season approaches, followed by an off-season or recovery phase. With regular testing (e.g. every four to six weeks), progress in response to a training program can be monitored and, where necessary, modifications to each player's program can be made.

General principles of testing

1. Tests should be sport-specific and assess those components of fitness (strength, endurance, speed, etc.) which have been identified as being important for the sport, game or activity. A combination of simple field tests (e.g. 1 RM bench press, vertical jump, 40 metre sprint, shuttle run) can often provide a comprehensive picture of a player's overall ability (RM refers to 'repetition maximum').

2. Tests should be reliable, repeatable and sensitive enough to allow detection of improvements in a player's fitness.

3. To improve the reliability of any given test, a standard protocol should be rigorously enforced. Not only must the method of administering the test be kept constant, but the time of day, prior warm-up and preceding test will all need to be identical across testing occasions to ensure that the results are meaningful and valid.

4. Testing should not be conducted so frequently that improvements in a given component of fitness can not be detected. Similarly, testing should be frequent enough for problems to be identified and for changes to be made to a particular training program in response. Testing every four to six weeks would be appropriate; this would involve a 3–5 week periodised training program followed by a 3 or 4 day rest period before testing. The testing period (including rest days prior to testing) can be used as a recovery period within the overall training program.

5. The order in which a battery of tests is administered should allow explosive tests (e.g. sprints) to be completed before endurance tests. An example of a week's testing could look like this:

Monday	Rest
Tuesday	Sprint and agility tests
Wednesday	Vertical jump and resistance tests
Thursday	Endurance tests
Friday	Rest
Saturday	Resumption of training

6. Players for whom particular tests are not relevant can be excluded from that component of testing. For example, a goal keeper in soccer might not be required to participate in a 5km time trial.

In addition to tests of physical ability, other tests which might be relevant to a particular sport include:

- Body composition (skinfolds, body weight)
- Podiatrical assessment (lower limb biomechanics, foot anatomy) by a sports podiatrist
- Dietary assessment by a sports dietitian
- Injury screening tests (including flexibility) by a sports physiotherapist
- Iron status by a sports physician
- Vision testing (standard and functional) by an optometrist

Establishing objectives and goals

Once the requirements of the game or the event have been established and the fitness level of the athlete involved is known through specific testing, goals need to be set. Individual goals for each player are important, not only for the player's motivation but also to provide specific direction during the pre-season training phase.

In a team sport, collective goals such as specifying averages for various tests which the group as a whole must achieve can help foster team spirit. Advantages of collective goal-setting include highlighting the contribution of those players who improve the most and who have therefore increased the average the most, in addition to providing a team focus at a time when the team is not competing.

PRE-SEASON TRAINING—GENERAL PREPARATION

Endurance

Aerobic capacity needs to be developed early in the pre-season. For this reason, the endurance work required here may initially be non-specific when compared to actual game requirements. Running is typically of the long continuous type and of low intensity, and may be supplemented during the early pre-season by cycling, swimming, boxing, or indeed any activity using large muscle groups which can be performed aerobically. A number of factors must be considered before prescribing endurance training. These include:

Training age: Individuals who have been competing for a number of years may require less 'base running' and be able to progress to more intense exercise to gain improvements in endurance fitness. Testing will identify those who can move into other training phases. An athlete whose endurance fitness is good may benefit from spending more time on other areas of fitness (e.g. flexibility). Remember the law of diminishing returns. For example, could the five hours a week required to achieve a 2% improvement in endurance performance with a naturally talented endurance athlete be as beneficial as investing five hours a week to gain a 10% improvement in an area of weakness (e.g. speed)?

Injuries: Older players in team sports may have cumulative joint damage which makes year-round weight-bearing training inadvisable. Also, in many team sports, the athletes are much heavier than the typical runner. In both cases an excellent alternative to land running is deep-water running. Deep-water running requires a pool deep enough that the player cannot touch the bottom; a water-running vest or belt will be needed to assist with flotation. Players then reproduce their land running style while immersed in the water. Learning deep-water running requires feedback from an observer/coach, as many of the proprioceptive cues used in land running are lost in the water. The advantages of deep-water running include: use of the same muscles as land running, hence good specificity; similar intensity levels to land running, hence similar fitness benefits; and no load bearing, hence less chance of injury. Disadvantages are few, the main one being lack of eccentric contraction and hence significant muscle soreness on return to land running if the athlete has done no land running at all during the program.

Requirements of the event: Beware of developing fitness components just for the sake of training. A well trained athlete may possess all the physical attributes and abilities necessary to perform at the top level in a team sport. Improving such an athlete's physical performance levels only 1–2% may require the investment of many hours which could be better used improving the player's skills or game play.

Volume of endurance training: is determined by the athlete's current level of endurance fitness, the current volume of endurance training, time devoted to other areas of physical development and the goals to be achieved during a particular period of time. Some general rules which are useful in prescribing endurance training are:

1. Increase the volume of training by no more than 10% per week. A more conservative approach may involve increasing volume one week and consolidating the increase the following week (i.e. increasing volume every second week).
2. Increase only one training variable at a time (i.e. if volume is being increased, intensity should remain constant, and vice versa).
3. Set the endurance sessions in terms of *time* instead of distance. This reduces the temptation to try and run a set distance faster than before (which can result in non-adherence to prescribed intensities). It also allows for different levels of ability in a squad.

Intensity of endurance training: The intensity of pre-season endurance training should not be too high; heart rate is the best way of prescribing intensity. The heart rate at the blood or plasma lactate inflection point determines the heart rate level for base endurance training. This involves determining blood lactate and heart rate during an incremental exercise protocol in such a way that a plot of velocity and heart rate vs lactate is developed (see Figure 3.3, p. 55).

If access to testing facilities (such as a university laboratory) is limited, a useful theoretical formula is 180 minus the *age of the athlete*, which, like all theoretical formulas, has a margin of error. For example, for a 25-year-old footballer with an inflection point on the lactate curve of 157 beats per minute (bpm), the optimum range for base endurance training would be 147–157 bpm. Using the theoretical formula 180–25 would give an intensity range of 145–155 bpm. Either way, the intensity of training early in the pre-season is kept low and is of quantifiable intensity.

Speed

The emphasis in speed training should be on sprinting technique and brief sprints (3–10 sec) with long recoveries (at least 60 seconds between efforts), in order to train the creatine phosphate energy system. Obviously, perfect running form will not be maintained in a team sport competition environment, but developing good running form during training will benefit both the musculoskeletal system (especially postural) and neural system (coordination and proprioception). It also allows coaches to detect running style deficiencies which may predispose an athlete to injury. In addition, the confidence that can be instilled in a player by sprinting well is a significant reason for including technique training in pre-season speed work.

Short sprints with long recoveries are valuable as they avoid fatiguing the player, who can then concentrate on technique while avoiding the chance of overtraining and becoming injured. It must be remembered that early pre-season is the time when most players have relatively low levels of fitness, which can leave them susceptible to becoming overtrained. Time lost to injury or illness at this time of the conditioning program is not worth the potential gains made by introducing high intensity training too early.

> ## TRAINING IS DESIGNED TO IMPROVE ATHLETES, NOT BREAK THEM DOWN

Guidelines for sprint training

1. The athlete must be fresh (non-fatigued) for sprint training to be most effective.
2. Afternoon or evening are the best times of day for sprint training (increased flexibility at the end of the day means less chance of injury and better performance).
3. A comprehensive warm-up is extremely important before a sprint session. It should include a gradual increase in intensity of running from jogging to sprinting as well as a full range of stretches.

Chapter 2 provides details of sprint technique and training sessions and advice.

Weight training

Weight training during the general pre-season phase centres around two main areas—*hypertrophy* (increased size) and *strength* of the muscles. The precise emphasis placed on these two components is determined by the requirements of individual athletes, which are in turn determined by their sport-specific duties. Young athletes with little weight training experience who need to gain size may stay in the hypertrophy phase of a weights program for most or all of their preparation. Older players who have achieved adequate size may benefit from concentrating more on strength development.

Typically, weight training which is aimed at improving size involves repetitions of between 8–15 lifts on any given weight. Emphasis is on slow, controlled contractions which place the muscles under tension for a prolonged period (e.g. 3 seconds down/eccentric, 2 seconds up/concentric). Strength training involves lifting heavier weights for 2–6 repetitions (sometime single lifts) to maximise muscle fibre recruitment. Emphasis is on a more explosive movement and on just completing the lift (though not at the expense of technique).

Table 4.1: A sample week in the general preparation phase for a games player						
Mon	**Tue**	**Wed**	**Thu**	**Fri**	**Sat**	**Sun**
End	Rest or Flex	End	Rest or Flex	End	Rest or Flex	Rest
Wts & Flex	Sprints Skills	Wts & Flex	Sprints Skills	Wts & Flex	End or Sprints	Rest
Notes: End = endurance; Wts = weights; Flex = flexibility						

Guidelines for weight training

1. Always warm up well with a 10 minute *low* intensity aerobic activity (e.g. walk/jog/bike/row/stepper) to raise body temperature, followed by specific stretches and at least 2 warm-up sets in the early major exercises.

2. *Never* sacrifice technique in order to lift a heavier weight or achieve an extra repetition. Correct technique in the gym affords better muscle development, ensures athletes are developing the muscles they are trying to train, decreases injury risk and ensures better development of the joint-stabilising muscles.

Injury

The other major focus of weight training in the general pre-season phase is injury rehabilitation and injury prevention. Players who suffered injuries during the previous season or who have a history of intrinsic or overuse injuries need to be given specific programs to correct weaknesses. For example, those athletes who repeatedly sprain their ankles will benefit from ankle joint strengthening, balance and proprioceptive training.

If hamstring tears or strains are a problem it is important to identify the cause: weakness or tightness, muscle imbalance or deficiencies in other areas, e.g. lower back. A program to remedy these problems can then be implemented. Input from a sports physiotherapist is recommended in the development of rehabilitative and preventative programs.

In addition, all the players may perform certain exercises to prevent the more common injuries in their sport. For example football players can use eccentric hamstring exercises to prevent hamstring tears or strains and rotator cuff strengthening exercises to prevent shoulder injuries.

SPECIFIC PREPARATION

Endurance

During the phase of specific preparation which precedes the start of the season, *specificity* is particularly important. Time and motion analyses and heart rate data are invaluable at this time. In general, endurance sessions in this phase should be designed to replicate the requirements of the event, but can be varied by developing sessions which reproduce game intensity with the same work/rest ratio; are above game intensity, by either increasing work or decreasing rest; or are below game intensity, by either decreasing work or increasing rest.

As an example, time-motion analysis may establish that a player covers 4km per 20-minute quarter (25–30 minutes real time) with the average sprint being approximately 20m. An endurance training session based on this data could follow one of these three patterns:

1. Match intensity session = 40 × 20m sprint with 80m jog, starting a sprint every 40–45 seconds.
2. Above match intensity = 40 × 20m with 80m jog, starting a sprint every 25–30 seconds *or* 20 × 200m in 35 seconds with 25 seconds walk.
3. Below-match intensity = 30 × 20m sprint with 80m jog, starting every minute.

As a general rule only one session per week should be above match intensity (MI), with one or two sessions per week at MI and two or more sessions per week below MI.

Example: 6 weeks of specific preparation

Weeks 1 & 2: 3–4 endurance sessions per week
    2–3 sessions below MI; 1 session at MI

Weeks 3 & 4: 3–4 endurance sessions per week
2 sessions below MI; 1–2 sessions at MI
Weeks 5 & 6: 3–4 endurance sessions per week
1 session below MI; 1–2 sessions at MI; 1 session above MI

Speed

The emphasis of speed development work during specific preparation is on the ability to repeat speed and on improving match-specific speed and agility.

Repeatable-speed sessions at this stage often blend with endurance sessions, especially for endurance-based players (e.g. a match intensity session in the endurance section could also be considered a session in which repeatable speed is developed). For less endurance-based positions repeatable speed may be improved by a maximal effort over a short relevant distance followed by one or two short efforts with little recovery (followed by a much longer recovery before repeating the drill). The kind of players who benefit from this include the forward-scoring player who has to lead for a pass at maximum speed and then double back rapidly if the ball is deflected or passed elsewhere, and then has a relatively long recovery period before the next effort. An example of this kind of drill: Sprint 40m maximally, stop briefly (less than one second), then sprint 20m either left, right or behind, then walk back to start at own pace. Repeat every 60–80 seconds.

Match-specific speed and agility is concerned with developing the ability to accelerate from different positions (e.g. slow jog, kneeling, lying down) and the ability to stop, start and change directions rapidly, especially when running at top speed. Drills where a coach is calling changes of direction to which the athlete has to respond as rapidly as possible are valuable match-specific training techniques; set agility courses allow the athletes to improve their turning ability without having to react to external stimuli.

Table 4.2:	A sample week in the specific preparation phase for the games player					
Mon	**Tue**	**Wed**	**Thu**	**Fri**	**Sat**	**Sun**
End <MI	Rest or Flex	End <MI	Rest or Flex	Rest or Flex	Rest or Flex	Rest
Wts	Speed/ Agility Skills	Wts	Repeat Speed = End at MI Skills	Wts	End MI or >MI	Rest

Notes: End = endurance; Wts = weights; Flex = flexibility MI = match intensity

Agility courses

The course should be sport specific i.e. lateral vs backward vs accelerate/decelerate.

Weight training

Weight training during the specific preparation phase should aim to convert the strength gained in the earlier phase of training into sport-specific power. Weight sets using 30–50% of 1RM (repetition maximum) and completing these as rapidly as possible will improve power. Weight training exercises aimed at injury prevention should also be maintained throughout this period.

COMPETITION PHASE

Due to the length of the competitive season in many team sports, recovery must be a high priority throughout the competition phase. Ensuring that players, and hence the team, recover from session to session and week to week, so that enough games are won to achieve a finals berth, is of great importance. Thus the emphasis must be on maintaining the conditioning levels achieved throughout the pre-season while at the same time allowing the players to peak for, and recover from, important matches.

Preventing injury, maximising recovery and hence increasing the number of games played is the best way to develop match fitness and improve the overall development of the team sport athlete.

Endurance

During the season, the weekend match can be considered the match-intensity endurance session for the week (following the specific preparation described above). The balance between maintaining endurance fitness and allowing recovery will determine how much other endurance training is performed each week. Actual skills training can often be considered a low intensity endurance training session that incorporates sport-specific speed work. For this reason the only other running-only session may be a short 10–15 minute endurance/repeated speed session which is above MI. The specific preparation pattern of one session at MI, one session above MI and one or more sessions below MI can therefore be carried over into the competition phase.

Speed

Once again, the actual game each week and skills training provide much, if not all, of the sport-specific speed work for the player; thus the only other speed training required is the maintenance of sprint technique and strength via the use of drill work. Drills such as high knees, heels to buttocks and alternate leg bounding for distance can be used to reinforce sprint technique. These drills can be incorporated into pre-training warm-ups two to three times each week. For those players who require strength maintenance, towing drills with a weighted sled are useful. Towing training should be done at most once each week, preferably early in the week.

Weights

One or two weight sessions per week should be adequate during the season. One session per week should be specifically aimed at maintaining strength (i.e. low reps, high resistance), while the other session may be more power oriented. Of the two, the strength-maintenance session is the more important. Exercises aimed at preventing injuries should

Table 4.3: A sample competition week training for the games player						
Mon	**Tue**	**Wed**	**Thu**	**Fri**	**Sat**	**Sun**
Recovery Water Work	Speed &/or End Wts	Skills End < MI	Rest or Wts	Skills	Rest	Game

Notes: MI = match intensity; End = endurance; Wts = weight training
Flexibility at all sessions.

be maintained throughout the competitive season. Players who have been injured should *continue* their rehabilitative exercises after their return to play as scar tissue remodelling can continue for up to six months after the injury.

Allowing for individual rates of recovery is extremely important during the competition phase, especially in team sports. Players who never miss a game or training session, or who play in particularly demanding positions, should have recovery weeks scheduled into their program to prevent overtraining, which can result in injury or illness.

No matter how skilled an individual, the contribution of complete conditioning to performance and injury prevention cannot be underestimated. A well conditioned games player will maintain a higher skill level for longer in addition to making fewer fatigue-induced judgment errors. Periodisation of the conditioning program is essential in producing the best result during the playing season. An individual who trains too hard too early and who peaks before the season starts has an uphill battle to maintain form during a competitive season of 20-plus weeks.

SUMMARY

- 'Event requirements' will determine the emphasis placed on an athlete during training. 'Match analysis' allows a coach and athlete to assess the event requirements and to devise training programs which target specialist playing positions.

- Fitness testing forms the cornerstone of any training program and athletes should first be tested at the start of the pre-season training period. Testing should then follow every four to six weeks.
- For most games players, endurance will need to be developed early in the pre-season training period. The type and volume of endurance training will depend on the training age, injury history and playing position of the athlete.
- Weight training in the pre-season period should progress from hypertrophy, to strength, to power training. Technique should be maintained throughout all sessions and training should always focus on quality rather than quantity.
- Training during the season should ensure maintenance of endurance, strength and speed.

RECOMMENDED READING

Baechle, T. R. (ed.), (1994) *Essentials of Strength Training and Conditioning* Human Kinetics, Champaign, Illinois.

Jenkins, D. (ed.), (1995) *The Level II Sports Science Manual* Australian Rugby Football Union, Sydney.

Rushall, B. and F. Pyke, (1990) *Training for Sports and Fitness* Macmillan, Melbourne.

5

Periodisation of speed and endurance training

Dr Brian Dawson

Periodisation is no more than a technical term for adopting a sensible and well planned approach to training, which maximises training gains and performance improvement. If maximising performance is not the goal, why do all the training in the first place? While having to plan ahead might seem like a chore, the alternative is usually an *ad hoc* approach which guarantees less than optimal improvement.

Success in sport these days is harder to achieve than it was perhaps 20 or 30 years ago. With our ever increasing knowledge of the energy requirements of various sports and responses to different types of training, it is now much less likely that the naturally gifted athlete will succeed on talent alone, as talent alone will not compensate for a poor or incomplete preparation. The key to success is a well organised training program, sometimes formulated years in advance of a major competition (e.g. the Olympics), which plans the training workouts on a daily, weekly, monthly and perhaps yearly basis. This approach allows a logical and sensible progression in the athlete's training load.

Periodisation involves dividing the training year (or season) into different phases. During each phase one or more of the physical demands of the event or game (e.g. endurance, strength, speed) is emphasised, depending on the dates of major competitions. Lower intensity base training is performed several months before important meets or games, but as the competition draws closer, higher intensity and more specific training must be undertaken.

PLANNING THE YEARLY TRAINING PROGRAM

The three main training phases in any annual training plan are the preparation (pre-season) phase; the competition (in-season) phase; and the transition (off-season) phase.

The *preparation phase* is normally divided into general and specific preparation sub-phases. Similarly, the *competition phase* is also further divided into pre-competitive and competitive sub-phases, as the types of training performed and the overall training load for each of the sub-phases must vary depending on forthcoming competition demands. Each of the phases and sub-phases is composed of smaller cycles (periods of time) in order to make the organisation and planning of the training program more systematic and manageable. These cycles are called macrocycles and microcycles. A macrocycle is usually one month (3–5 weeks) in length while a microcycle is typically one week in length, such that 3–5 microcycles make up one macrocycle.

Each of the macrocycles and microcycles has specific objectives for the development of certain abilities in the athlete (e.g. speed, strength, flexibility, skill) which fit with the overall objectives for each of the training phases. Table 5.1 presents the training year with its divisions into the various phases and cycles.

The length of the respective phases and sub-phases will vary between different sports. For example, many team sports (e.g. football, hockey, basketball) have a six to eight month competition phase, whereas track and field athletes may only compete seriously for four or five months. The summer months will be the transition and preparation phases for football and rugby players, but will be the competition phase for cricketers, sprinters and jumpers. When planning the yearly training program it is wise to

Table 5.1: The training year, divided into its various phases, sub-phases and cycles

The yearly plan

Phases of training	Preparation			Competition						Transition		
Sub-phases	General preparation		Specific prep-aration	Pre-competitive	Competitive					Transition		
Macro-cycles (months)	1	2	3	4	5	6	7	8	9	10	11	12
Micro-cycles (weeks)	1 2 3 4 5 6 7 8		9 10 11 12 13 14 15 16 17	18 19 20 21 22	23 24 25 26 27 28	29 30 31 32 33 34	35 36 37 38	39 40 41 42 43 44 45	46 47 48 49 50 51 52			

work backwards from the date of the most important competition, and organise the phases and cycles of the training year according to this calendar date.

A typical macrocycle

Table 5.2 presents an example of a macrocycle for an endurance runner who is just beginning the general preparation sub-phase of training (see Table 5.1). There are six training sessions (four running and two weights sessions) planned for each microcycle, and four microcycles make up a macrocycle.

The types of training used reflect the phase of training; in this example the athlete is just beginning to prepare for the next competitive season, therefore the objective of this macrocycle would be to develop an endurance base of fitness. Hence, endurance base training is programmed.

After the first two microcycles, however, more intensive (interval training and anaerobic threshold) training workouts are gradually introduced, in preparation for future macrocycles. The training sessions are spaced over the week such that there is no more than one session per day and the athlete has to run on consecutive days only once (Friday and Saturday). This is designed to allow for sufficient recovery time between training sessions, so that the athlete does not become tired and stale from too much training. With this in mind, the seventh training session for the week is a planned recovery day, where the athlete does no formal training and may use massage, spa, nutritional repletion and/or other recovery techniques to overcome the fatigue induced by the training sessions and start fresh for the next week's training.

Recovery days should be programmed, and considered as training sessions themselves, and the reasons for their presence in the training program should be made clear to the athletes. Many athletes, with the best of intentions, will see a recovery day as an opportunity to squeeze in an extra training session; often the coach will have no knowledge of

Table 5.2: A typical macrocycle for an endurance runner at the beginning of the general preparation sub-phase of training

Type of training	Days																											
	M	T	W	Th	F	Sa	S	M	T	W	Th	F	Sa	S	M	T	W	Th	F	Sa	S	M	T	W	Th	F	Sa	S
Low intensity aerobic training	X	X	X	X	X	X		X		X		X	X		X		X		X			X		X		X		
Fartlek training																	X			X				X				
Anaerobic threshold training																											X	
Endurance weight training		X		X					X		X					X		X					X		X			
Recovery days							X							X							X							X
Objectives	Develop base endurance							Develop base endurance							Develop base endurance							Develop base endurance						
	Minimise muscle soreness in first week							20% increase in weekly km.							Introduce Fartlek training for pace change							Introduce anaerobic threshold training for higher quality						
															Increase reps by 5 for weight training													
	Microcycle 1							Microcycle 2							Microcycle 3							Microcycle 4						

this, and the long-term effect may well be a tired and over-trained athlete.

A typical microcycle

The microcycle is the hub of the training program as it involves all the training sessions for the week. As a general rule, only one or two microcycles should be planned in advance, as the rate and degree of improvement by different athletes cannot always be accurately predicted. In contrast, the macrocycle should be planned in advance, although more or less microcycles than originally thought may be needed to meet its objectives. Here coaches and athletes need to be flexible and sensible in conducting the training program.

Table 5.3 presents an example of a microcycle for a 100-metre sprinter in the competition phase of training who has a weekend club meet. The objective of this microcycle is to maintain the speed and power developed in the previous macrocycles and microcycles, and also to improve start, relay changeover and running technique, while allowing sufficient recovery pre-competition.

There are two morning (AM) weight training sessions, with the heavier loads and greater volume occurring earlier in the week (Tuesday), and the lighter loads and lesser volume being programmed later in the week (Thursday), which is closer to the competition day. The Monday and Wednesday afternoon (PM) sessions are the harder track workouts, with the Tuesday and Thursday PM sessions emphasising skill and technique more than conditioning. There are three half-day recovery sessions programmed (Monday, Wednesday and Friday AM), with a full day of recovery both preceding and following the competition day. Also, the harder PM sessions are separated by an easier PM Tuesday workout, as programming high intensity workouts on consecutive days is inappropriate.

To allow sufficient recovery and enable athletes to perform quality workouts without being restricted by residual fatigue from earlier training sessions, at least one day of recovery or easier training should always separate the hardest

Table 5.3: A typical microcycle for a 100-metre sprinter during the competition phase of training

	Monday	Tuesday	Wednesday	Thursday	Friday	Saturday	Sunday
AM	Recovery	*Power weight training* 3 × 4 Squat—85% 1RM 2 × 12 Bench step ups—30kg bar 3 × 4 Bench press 85% 1RM 3 × 12 Hip extension 3 × 6 Lat pulldown 80% 1RM 3 × 8 Leg curl—75% 1RM	Recovery	*Power weight training* 3 × 10 Squat—60% 1RM 3 × 8 Box jumps 1.2m 3 × 6 Cleans 70% 1RM 2 × 15 Medicine ball catch & throw—7kg	Recovery	Recovery	Recovery Low intensity aerobic training 4–5 km easy
PM	*Plyometrics* 2 × 6 Double leg long jumps 3 × 6 Hurdle jumps 2 × 30 metres Bounding *Maximal alactic anaerobic training* 6 × 60 metres on 5 min. (max. speed) 3 × 150 metres on 8 min. (95% max. speed)	*Low intensity aerobic training* Jog curves, 50% max. speed stride in straights for 5 laps Technique drills for 15–20 minutes (at ≈75% max. speed)	*Maximal alactic anaerobic training* 2 sets of 4 × 75 metres (max. speed) 5 min. between reps 10 min between sets 2km easy jog	*Maximal alactic anaerobic training* 6 × 30 metres (blocks starts) on 3 min. 6 × 50 metres (baton change) on curve on 4 min. (max. speed) 2km easy jog	Recovery	*Competition* 100 metres 4 × 100 metres relay	Recovery

training workouts in a microcycle. Furthermore, no more than two high intensity sessions should be programmed in any one microcycle, as this may overload the athlete and reduce the expected improvement in performance.

PLANNING A TRAINING SESSION

To achieve maximum effect, each training session must be planned in advance and designed to fit into the overall objectives of the current microcycle. This, however, does not mean that each training session directly promotes the main objective of the microcycle. For example, a low intensity aerobic training session, separating two maximal alactic anaerobic training sessions, does not directly work to improve speed and power for a sprinter, which may be the main objective of the microcycle. The easy aerobic session is just as important as the more specific sprint workouts in achieving overall objectives, as it helps to facilitate good recovery between the intense training sessions, without which it is unlikely that the same degree of improvement could occur.

Once again, it is important to understand that easier training sessions and recovery sessions are fundamental to improvement in performance. High intensity training workouts cannot be performed every day and should not be programmed more than twice a week. Therefore, in planning a training session, the type of training to be performed should be determined by considering:

- the main objectives of the microcycle
- the date of the next competition
- yesterday's training
- tomorrow's training.

The structure of a training session

Each training session can be split into various segments and should be conducted such that the training activities are

Table 5.4: The various segments of a training session for a team game player	
Minutes	
0	1. Team briefing (5 min.)
5	2. Warm-up (15 min.)
20	3. Speed, power training (10 min.)
30	4. Individual and team skill drills (50 min.)
80	5. Special skill or fitness training (15 min.)
95	6. Cool-down (5 min.)
100	

performed in a logical sequence. The correct ordering of training activities is important in order to avoid one training activity reducing the effectiveness of another. An example of incorrect ordering would be the programming of fine skill work for a footballer immediately after completing an intense period of repeated short sprints which produce a high blood lactic acid level. A suggested order of training activities for a team game player is as follows:

1. Team briefing—to set the tone for the training session.
2. General warm-up—easy aerobic exercise, then stretching.
3. Speed or power training—best done while fresh.
4. Individual and team skill drills—incorporating tactics and strategies.
5. Specialised fitness and/or skill work—depending on individual player requirements
6. Cool down—easy aerobic exercise, then stretching.

An example of the structure of a training session for a team game, divided into its various segments is given in Table 5.4.

For speed athletes the order of training activities may be simplified even further:

1. General warm-up.
2. Speed and power training.
3. Technique training.
4. Specific fitness and conditioning training.
5. Cool down.

For endurance athletes only three training activities may be required:

1. General warm-up.
2. Specific fitness and conditioning training.
3. Cool down.

It is also possible that not all of the listed activities will be used in each training session, depending on the objectives of the microcycle.

PERIODISATION OF THE TRAINING YEAR

The preparation (pre-season) phase

The prime objective of the preparation phase for any athlete is to develop a sound fitness base on which the more intense and specialised training for competition can be built. The longer the base period of training the more easily the athlete should be able to adapt and respond to high intensity training. Furthermore, the longer the period of base training the longer the athlete should be able to perform consistently at her/his peak during the competition phase. Hence, the preparation phase usually involves two or three macrocycles, one or two in the general preparation sub-phase and one in the specific preparation sub-phase. The first macrocycle typically involves a high volume of low to moderate intensity training, which is progressively and gradually reversed in nature over the remainder of this phase (i.e. lower volume and higher intensity training).

While endurance, speed and team game athletes all have different specific competition energy requirements, they can all benefit from developing a good endurance base of fitness. Because this is directly related to performance for an endurance athlete, speed and team game athletes will find that good endurance fitness will enhance their recovery from high intensity training efforts, which will be performed in future macrocycles. A greater number of quality repeats in a training set should also be possible before undue fatigue occurs. Team game players such as Australian Rules footballers and soccer players may cover 10–20 km in total distance during a game, which may last from 70–120 min, further emphasising the need to develop good endurance fitness.

However, the training methods used to build endurance will vary with the type of athlete. While continuous aerobic training is appropriate for an endurance athlete, speed athletes should use higher intensity interval training, where the type II (fast twitch) muscle fibres which are more specific to their competition requirements will be recruited and used. If the endurance base is achieved mostly by lower intensity continuous aerobic training, the type I (slow twitch) muscle fibres will be preferentially recruited, which may be counterproductive to the speed and power development of a sprint athlete. Team game players may use a mix of continuous and interval training, as this is more suited to their specific game requirements.

As well as developing an endurance base of fitness, speed and team game players must also develop strength and power by appropriate weight training during the preparation phase. While power development is the ultimate goal for speed athletes especially, increases in strength are fundamental to improvements in power, which will then be emphasised in the competition phase.

Many contact team sports (e.g. football) also require improvements in strength for injury prevention and greater force generation in tackling, blocking and bumping. Here, coaches and athletes should be aware that concurrent strength (or speed) and endurance training may interfere with each other. That is, if both of these capacities are trained together, then the overall improvement in each of them is likely to be less than if they were trained separately. This is most likely due to differences in the pattern and efficiency of muscle fibre recruitment, as endurance training utilises mostly type I fibres, while high intensity strength (or speed) training utilises type II (as well as type I) fibres. In practice, to avoid seriously compromising the degree of improvement in either capacity, the following points should be borne in mind: don't attempt to train strength/speed and endurance in the same session or day; separate days (at the least) should be used. In any macrocycle, the development of either strength/speed or

Table 5.5: Training methods for use in the preparation phase for endurance, speed and team game athletes

Type of athlete	Preparation phase	
	General preparation sub-phase	Specific preparation sub-phase
Endurance	low intensity aerobic training (more)	low intensity aerobic training (less)
	fartlek training	fartlek training
	anaerobic threshold training (less)	anaerobic threshold training (more)
	endurance weight training	endurance weight training
	flexibility training	flexibility training
	recovery training (massage, spa, etc.)	recovery training
Speed	alactic anaerobic training (≈ 75% of max.)	alactic anaerobic training (80–100% max.)
	lactic anaerobic training (≈ 75% of max.)	lactic anaerobic training (80–90% max.)
	low intensity aerobic training (for recovery)	low intensity aerobic training (for recovery)
	strength and power weight training	strength and power weight training
	flexibility training	flexibility training
	recovery training	recovery training
Team game	low intensity aerobic training (more)	low intensity aerobic training (less)
	fartlek training	fartlek training
	maximal aerobic training (less)	maximal aerobic training (more)
	alactic anaerobic training (≈ 75% of max.) (less)	alactic anaerobic training (80–90% max.) (more)
	strength weight training	strength and power weight training
	individual skill training	individual and team skills training
	flexibility training	flexibility training
	recovery training	recovery training

endurance should be emphasised, while the other capacity is maintained by lesser amounts of training.

Lastly, team game players must also develop their basic skills during the preparation phase. Simple, individual skills should be trained first, before progressing to more complex and tactically oriented skills. Table 5.5 presents an outline of the training methods which are appropriate for use in the preparation phase for all three groups of athletes.

The competition (in-season) phase

The objective of the competition phase is to develop an athlete's specific fitness and readiness for competition to maximum levels. Training is of a high intensity with a gradually reducing volume as the competition date draws near. The pre-competition sub-phase (usually one macro-cycle), which immediately follows the specific preparation sub-phase, is possibly the most demanding period of training in the year. High intensity, quality training (at or very near race or game intensity) of moderate volume is performed in this macrocycle, to bring the athletes' specific fitness and skill requirements to their peak. For team game athletes, strategies and tactics to be used in competition must be emphasised and practised. The strength developed in the preparation phase for both team game and speed athletes must be converted into power by performing plyometric and power weight training.

This sub-phase of training is, therefore, a potentially stressful period for the athlete. Here the responses to, and recovery from, the training load must be objectively considered by coaches and athletes, as injuries and chronic fatigue must be avoided. The advice of Forbes Carlisle, the well respected Australian swimming coach of the 1950s, 1960s and 1970s should be heeded—it is better to under-train than to over-train.

The competitive sub-phase may last some months and therefore will incorporate several macrocycles. Fitness should be maintained in this period by specific high intensity training of relatively low volume. Redevelopment of specific fitness may be required for athletes who suffer injury. As fitness should be at its peak when entering this sub-phase, the focus of training can be directed more to skill, technique, tactics and psychology, and special attention should be paid to ensuring a good preparation for each competition.

The final microcycle before every competition should allow peaking to occur. Training workouts should be at or close to competition intensity, but be brief in duration and few in number, such that a low volume of training is performed. More recovery sessions should also be programmed and nutritional procedures such as carbohydrate loading emphasised. This type of macrocycle works well for endurance and speed athletes, who may have infrequent

Type of athlete	Competition phase	
	Pre-competition sub-phase	**Competition sub-phase**
Endurance	low intensity aerobic training	low intensity aerobic training (recovery)
	anaerobic threshold training	anaerobic threshold training
	maximal aerobic training	maximal aerobic training
	endurance weight training (maintain)	endurance weight training (maintain)
	flexibility training (maintain)	flexibility training (maintain)
	recovery training	recovery training plus peaking
Speed	maximal alactic anaerobic training	maximal alactic anaerobic training
	maximal lactic anaerobic training	maximal lactic anaerobic training
	low intensity aerobic training (for recovery)	low intensity aerobic training (for recovery)
	strength and power weight training	strength and power weight training
	flexibility training (maintain)	flexibility training (maintain)
	recovery training	recovery training plus peaking
Team game	low intensity aerobic training (for recovery)	low intensity aerobic training (for recovery)
	maximal aerobic training	maximal aerobic training
	maximal alactic anaerobic training	maximal alactic anaerobic training
	strength and power weight training	strength and power weight training
	individual and team skill training	individual and team skills training
	flexibility training (maintain)	flexibility training (maintain)
	recovery training	recovery training plus 'mini peaking'

Table 5.6: Training methods for use in the competition phase for endurance, speed and team game athletes

competitions scheduled, or are planning for major events such as state or national titles. Team game players are quite different; they must usually compete each week, with only a five to eight day break between games. Recovery and lower intensity training sessions should be programmed early in the week to allow sufficient recovery from the previous game. The main training session is performed midweek (moderate to high intensity and volume), with a brief quality workout taking place one or two days prior to the next game. Recovery and nutritional procedures (carbohydrate loading) should also be emphasised at this stage of the week.

Microcycles of this nature are designed to allow a mini peak for each game throughout the competition phase, but it is no easy matter to achieve this during weekly competition. A more

Table 5.7:	Training methods for use in the transition phase for endurance, speed and team game athletes	
Type of athlete	**Transition phase**
Endurance	low intensity aerobic training (cross training)
Speed	low intensity aerobic training (cross training) alactic anaerobic training (60–80% of max.) lactic anaerobic training (60–80% of max.) endurance weight training strength weight training
Team game	low intensity aerobic training (cross training) endurance weight training strength weight training

complete peaking cycle can sometimes be attempted in the finals series when a team has a relatively easy passage through to the grand final.

Table 5.6 presents training methods for use in the competition phase.

The transition (off-season) phase

The main objective of this phase is to prevent 'detraining' and maintain a reasonable level of endurance fitness, while accepting that some reduction in peak condition will occur. The transition phase is also a time when nagging injuries can recover, and coaches and athletes can psychologically benefit from a break in the normal training routine, especially after the additional stresses of the competition phase. Specific weaknesses in an athlete's profile (e.g. lack of flexibility, upper body strength or skill on non-preferred side) can also receive special attention without interference from other types of training.

To maintain some degree of endurance fitness and provide a break from normal training, the athlete can cross-train during the transition phase. Cycling, swimming, running, water running, rowing and team or individual games (basketball, touch football, squash and tennis) are examples of activities which can assist in maintaining endurance fitness and limiting any weight gain. These sorts of activities are most appropriate for the endurance and team game athletes, and while speed athletes may also use them, they should also perform some interval training (perhaps once a week) at reduced intensity (60–80% of max speed) to prevent total detraining (loss of fitness) of their type II muscle fibres. Endurance and/or strength weight training should also be performed once a week by speed and team game athletes to limit the decline in specific muscle conditioning.

The amount of training done during this phase will determine the planning of the first microcycle and macrocycle in the general preparation sub-phase of the next annual plan. Table 5.7 shows the training methods for use in the transition phase.

The annual training plan

To conclude this chapter it is appropriate to present some examples of annual training plans. While these plans may appear complicated, constructing such charts is useful for establishing a logical sequence for the development of the necessary fitness components for the required sport. Also, the integration of skills, tactics and psychology into the overall plan to coincide with the cycles of the physical training program and the dates of important competitions is possible, so that overloading can be avoided. It should be remembered that if an athlete cannot respond positively to a training program (i.e. one or two microcycles or a full macrocycle) because of general tiredness or fatigue, then the training program must be re-evaluated and the possible causes (apart from training overload) of the fatigue investigated.

Figures 5.1, 5.2 and 5.3 present examples of annual training plans for endurance, speed and team game athletes.

Figure 5.1: An example of an annual training plan for endurance athletes (southern hemisphere)

THE CHART OF THE ANNUAL PLAN   TYPE: YEAR: COACH:

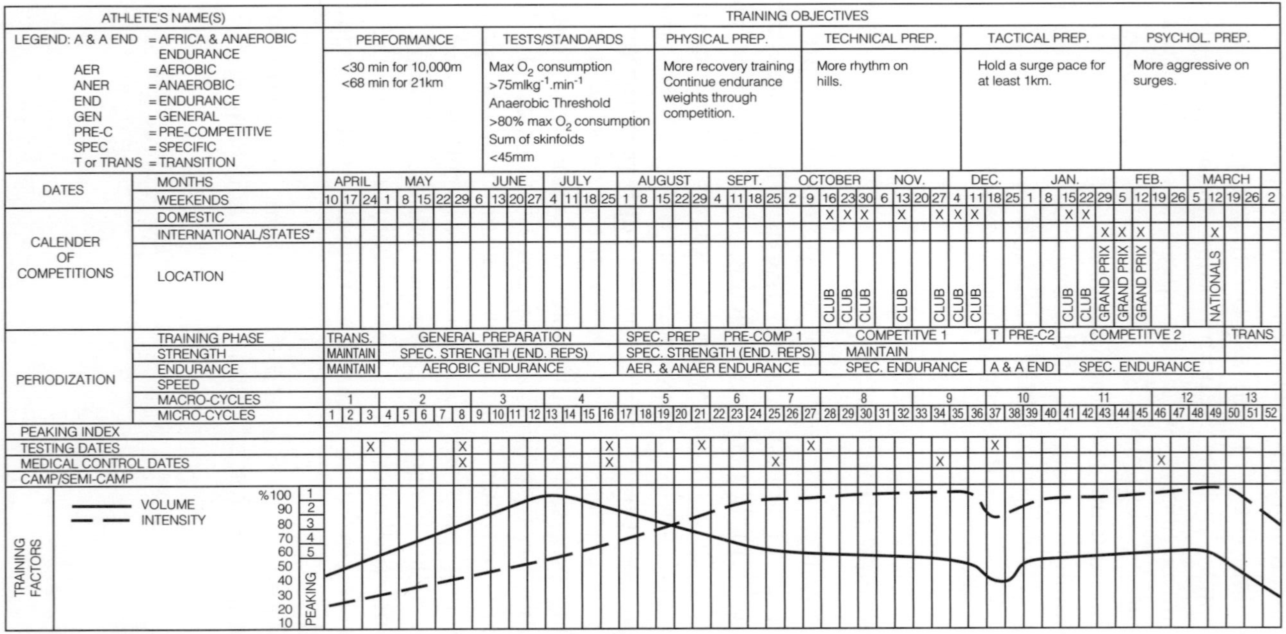

ATHLETE'S NAME(S)

LEGEND: A & A END = AFRICA & ANAEROBIC ENDURANCE
AER = AEROBIC
ANER = ANAEROBIC
END = ENDURANCE
GEN = GENERAL
PRE-C = PRE-COMPETITIVE
SPEC = SPECIFIC
T or TRANS = TRANSITION

TRAINING OBJECTIVES

PERFORMANCE	TESTS/STANDARDS	PHYSICAL PREP.	TECHNICAL PREP.	TACTICAL PREP.	PSYCHOL. PREP.
<30 min for 10,000m <68 min for 21km	Max O$_2$ consumption >75ml.kg^{-1}.min^{-1} Anaerobic Threshold >80% max O$_2$ consumption Sum of skinfolds <45mm	More recovery training Continue endurance weights through competition.	More rhythm on hills.	Hold a surge pace for at least 1km.	More aggressive on surges.

TRAINING FACTORS

Source: Design of chart taken from Tudor O. Bompa, *Theory and Methodology of Training*, 2nd edn, 1990.

Figure 5.2: An Example of an annual training plan for speed athletes (southern hemisphere)

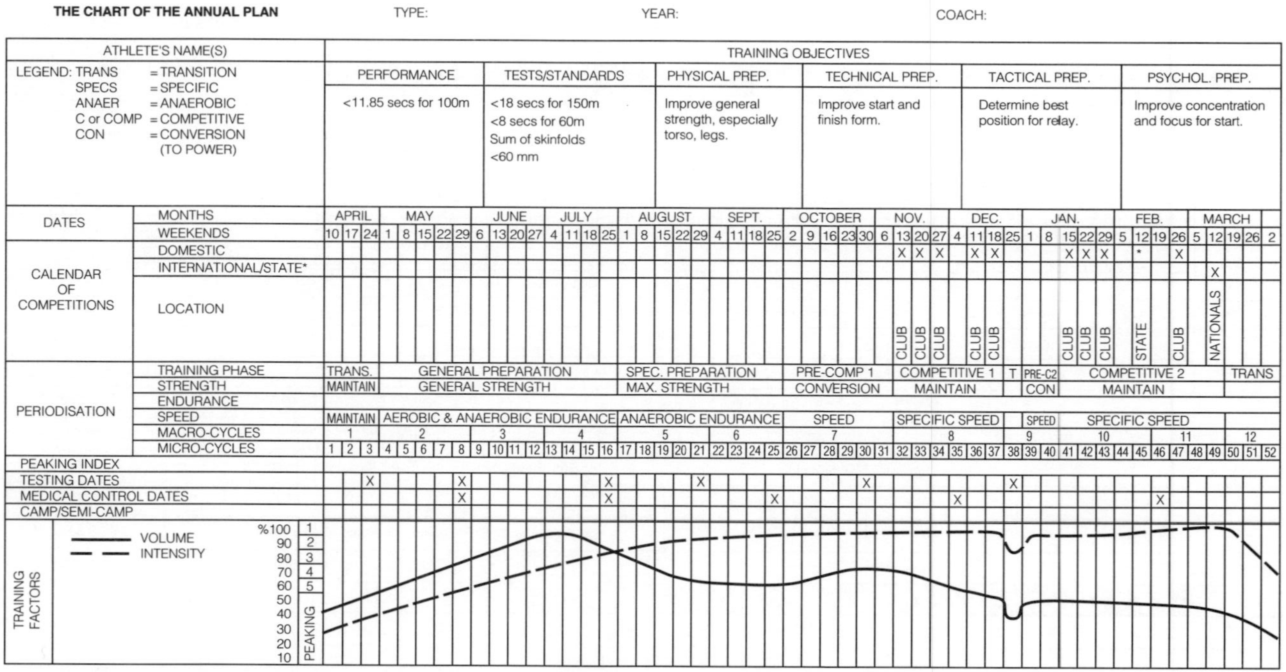
THE CHART OF THE ANNUAL PLAN
TYPE:
YEAR:
COACH:
ATHLETE'S NAME(S)
TRAINING OBJECTIVES
LEGEND: TRANS = TRANSITION
SPECS = SPECIFIC
ANAER = ANAEROBIC
C or COMP = COMPETITIVE
CON = CONVERSION (TO POWER)
PERFORMANCE
<11.85 secs for 100m
TESTS/STANDARDS
<18 secs for 150m
<8 secs for 60m
Sum of skinfolds <60 mm
PHYSICAL PREP.
Improve general strength, especially torso, legs.
TECHNICAL PREP.
Improve start and finish form.
TACTICAL PREP.
Determine best position for relay.
PSYCHOL. PREP.
Improve concentration and focus for start.
DATES
MONTHS
APRIL MAY JUNE JULY AUGUST SEPT. OCTOBER NOV. DEC. JAN. FEB. MARCH
WEEKENDS
10 17 24 1 8 15 22 29 6 13 20 27 4 11 18 25 1 8 15 22 29 4 11 18 25 2 9 16 23 30 6 13 20 27 4 11 18 25 1 8 15 22 29 5 12 19 26 5 12 19 26 2
CALENDAR OF COMPETITIONS
DOMESTIC
INTERNATIONAL/STATE*
LOCATION
CLUB CLUB CLUB CLUB CLUB CLUB CLUB CLUB STATE CLUB NATIONALS
PERIODISATION
TRAINING PHASE
TRANS. GENERAL PREPARATION SPEC. PREPARATION PRE-COMP 1 COMPETITIVE 1 T PRE-C2 COMPETITIVE 2 TRANS
STRENGTH
MAINTAIN GENERAL STRENGTH MAX. STRENGTH CONVERSION MAINTAIN CON MAINTAIN
ENDURANCE
SPEED
MAINTAIN AEROBIC & ANAEROBIC ENDURANCE ANAEROBIC ENDURANCE SPEED SPECIFIC SPEED SPEED SPECIFIC SPEED
MACRO-CYCLES
1 2 3 4 5 6 7 8 9 10 11 12
MICRO-CYCLES
1 2 3 4 5 6 7 8 9 10 11 12 13 14 15 16 17 18 19 20 21 22 23 24 25 26 27 28 29 30 31 32 33 34 35 36 37 38 39 40 41 42 43 44 45 46 47 48 49 50 51 52
PEAKING INDEX
TESTING DATES
MEDICAL CONTROL DATES
CAMP/SEMI-CAMP
TRAINING FACTORS
VOLUME
INTENSITY
%100 90 80 70 60 50 40 30 20 10
1 2 3 4 5
PEAKING

Source: Design of chart taken from Tudor O. Bompa, *Theory and Methodology of Training,* 2nd edn, 1990.

Figure 5.3: An example of an annual training plan for team game athletes (based on Australian football)

Annual training and competitive plan

Months	Nov	Dec	Jan	Feb	Mar	Apr	May	Jun	Jul	Aug	Sep	Oct
Competitions												
Periodisation	Preparation		Special prep.	Pre-season competition	Competition						Finals	Transition
Macrocycles	Conditioning	General basic		Specific basic				Unloading		Maintain	Peak	
Endurance	Aerobic capacity		Max aer power	Anaerobic alactic power		Anaerobic alactic capacity	Maintain					
Strength	General	Maximum		Power			Maintain					
Flexibility		Develop					Maintain					
Speed	Develop running speed					Develop movement speed		Maintain/develop rhythm and co-ordination				
Technique (skill)	Maintain basic Remedial		Improve basic	Acquire variants	Acquire advanced				Consolidate and synchronise			
Tactics (team play)	Maintain elementary Acquire advanced				Competition and motivation development			Refine and maintain			Spec. finals preparation	
Psychology	Assess basic skill Devel. Indiv programs		Specific mental skills									
Testing												
% Training time:												
Conditioning	70	60	50	40	30	20	20	20	20	30	20	
Skill	30	40	30	30	40	40	40	40	30	20	20	
Tactical	–	–	30	30	30	40	40	40	50	50	60	
Training load												

Training load: 100% / 80% / 60%

Legend: ⊠ In-season competition games ▨ Pre-season competition games ■ Grand final ◢ Semi finals ▩ Test dates
—— Volume - - - Intensity ▦ Test dates

Source: Lawrie Woodman and Frank Pyke *Sports Coach* Vol. 14, No. 2, 1991, pp. 32–9.

SUMMARY

- Periodisation is the process of organising training into a structured, manageable and scientifically sound arrangement of priorities.
- Generally, irrespective of the period over which the athlete intends to plan his/her training, there are three phases: the preparation phase, the competition phase and the transition phase.
- Once the 'big picture' has been planned (which may involve deciding on the relative emphases of, for example, strength, speed and endurance training), the athlete and/or coach must attend to the details of day-to-day training sessions.
- Especially important, and often neglected, is the need to periodise sessions to focus on injury prevention and recovery. Moreover, if the periodised plan is simply failing to produce the expected results, then the coach and athlete must re-evaluate their approach and change the plan.
- The competition phase requires the athlete to maintain fitness, often over several months. This must be carefully balanced against coping with the stresses of competition (and avoiding overtraining) and the need to taper before competition.
- In the off-season (i.e. the transition phase), athletes should prevent a loss of their fitness while having a mental break from their particular sport. Cross training during this phase is ideal, particularly if nagging injuries can be allowed to recover while general fitness is maintained.

RECOMMENDED READING

Bompa, Tudor O. (1987) 'Periodisation as a key element of planning', in *Sports Coach,* Vol. 11, No. 1, pages 20–23.

Bompa, Tudor, O. (2nd edn 1990) *Theory and Methodology of Training (the Key to Athletic Performance)* Kendall Hunt Publishing Company, Dubuque, Iowa.

Meir, R. (1993) *A Model for the Integration of Macrocycle and Microcycle Structure in Professional Rugby League*, in The Australian Strength and Conditioning Association Collective Articles Series, Australian Strength and Conditioning Association, Brisbane.

Pyke, F. S. (ed.) (1991) *Better Coaching*, Australian Coaching Council, Canberra, (in particular Chapter 17).

Rushall, B. S. and F. S. Pyke (1990) *Training for Sports and Fitness*, Macmillan, Melbourne.

Woodman, L. and F. S. Pyke, (1991) 'Periodisation of Australian football training', in *Sports Coach*, Vol. 14, No. 2, pages 32–39.

6

Recovery training

Angie Calder

If athletes want to be the best at their chosen sport then there is no alternative to hard work. But training hard and training smart are not always the same thing. Unless there is a corresponding adaptation to the type of training undertaken, the physical and psychological demands placed on an athlete can lead to overtraining, overuse or burnout problems. Any athlete unlucky enough to experience any of these conditions can quite easily feel that all their hard work has been a waste of time and effort. For many athletes the question becomes, 'How can I train hard without falling apart?' If athletes want to perform at their best without experiencing these problems they need to follow the formula for success:

WORK HARD + RECOVER WELL = BEST PERFORMANCE

Many athletes work hard but too often ignore recovery activities except when they are ill or injured, yet recovery training is an essential ingredient of a balanced training program. Indeed, together with overload and specificity, recovery is one of the basic principles of training, but it is the one most frequently forgotten in training programs.

THE PRINCIPLE OF RECOVERY

Training alone will not achieve the best results. An athlete needs time to adapt to the work undertaken. The principle of recovery refers to that part of the training process where the benefits of training are maximised through practices which encourage natural adaptation to the training stimulus.

Training sessions are designed to bring about improvements in athletic performance. This is achieved in part through progressively overloading the body and the fuel stores which underpin each of the five S's of training (stamina, strength, speed, suppleness and skill). Underlying this progressive overload principle is the understanding that in order to develop a particular capacity or system, that capacity must first be challenged or stressed. This stress is provided by the training load which represents the stimulus for change to occur. The work undertaken results in a degree of fatigue or depletion of the physical or psychological systems involved. Adaptation to training is accelerated when fatigued systems are restored to normal operational levels as quickly as possible after training.

Adaptation to the stimuli or workload is evidenced by improved performance which is the goal of every training program. Positive adaptation to a training stimulus is sometimes referred to as 'overcompensation'. The principle of recovery relates to the encouragement of adaptive processes after the presentation of the training stimulus. If there is sufficient recovery before the next workload the underlying system or fuel store stressed during training can improve its capacity to cope with the next stressor. Planning appropriate recovery activities as part of the training program accelerates adaptation to the training stimuli by reducing the time it takes for an athlete to reach the overcompensated state referred to in Figure 6.1.

OVERTRAINING, OVERUSE AND BURNOUT

If positive adaptation to training results in improved performances then recognising that negative adaptation can also occur is vital. Essentially, the high number of overtraining

Figure 6.1: Accelerated adaptation through accelerated recovery

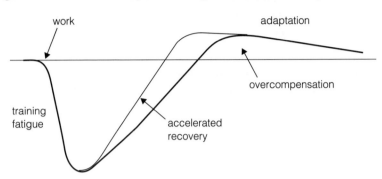

signs and symptoms reflect the wide ranging influence of the athlete's immune system when it is unable to cope with excessive stress of training. Overuse problems are an indication of biomechanical dysfunction due to excessive or inefficient loading patterns, and burnout occurs when athletes are so psychologically drained they lose motivation and often also lose all interest in their sport.

The onset of these conditions is diverse and varied. No two athletes will respond to training loads in the same way. Adaptation rates vary from one individual to another so it is not always appropriate to prescribe the same workloads for athletes in the same area; it is essential to monitor individual responses to training so that workloads can be varied accordingly. The wise coach will monitor an athlete's responses through cues or signs that are indicative of non-adaptive responses to training (Table 6.1). The coach's observations should include both sport-specific and basic cues.

MONITORING TRAINING RESPONSES

The responsible athlete should monitor training adaptations through regular recordings in a training diary or log book. This is an essential tool for all athletes, who must learn how to read themselves. Learning to listen to the body's signs and cues is one of the most important skills an athlete can acquire. Recordings of the quality of sleep, morning resting

Table 6.1: A coach's observations of the athlete's adaptation to training	
Coaching observations	**Signs and symptoms of non-adaptation**
Direct communication	Athletes tell me that: • they have heavy legs • they don't feel good • their legs are sore • they are tired
Body language	Facial expression and colour The look in their eyes Bending over to recover after an effort Bad technique compared to normal
Physiological	Increase in resting heart rate Loss of body weight Loss of appetite
Psychological	Low motivation Low concentration Aggressiveness No self-confidence
Others	Poor eating habits Poor sleep patterns
Source: From Guy Thibault (1993), Canadian speed skating coach.	

heart rate and morning body weight, and a daily rating of fatigue levels, are four critical markers that should be recorded every day (Figures 6.2 and 6.3).

One of the first signs of overtraining is consistently poor sleep patterns. An elevated resting heart rate recorded first thing in the morning (i.e. more than 6–10 beats per minute above the normal range) is an indication that any training undertaken should be minimal if at all. Body weight, best recorded each morning before eating and after going to the toilet, is not a measure of fat stores but may be an indication of body water levels. Rapid weight loss or rapid weight gain is not advisable, and unexplained weight loss may be indicative of overstress. Feeling tired after training is a normal response but feeling fatigued all the time is a sign that the body has not adapted to its stressors. These four markers take two minutes a day to record; variations in them may be the first indication of maladaptation or non-adaptation to training (Figure 6.2).

Many coaches are frustrated by the lack of consistency with which these variables are recorded by many athletes. Some athletes choose to ignore signs of any kind so they do not keep any records, diary or training log despite

Figure 6.2: Instructions for the self-monitoring sheet

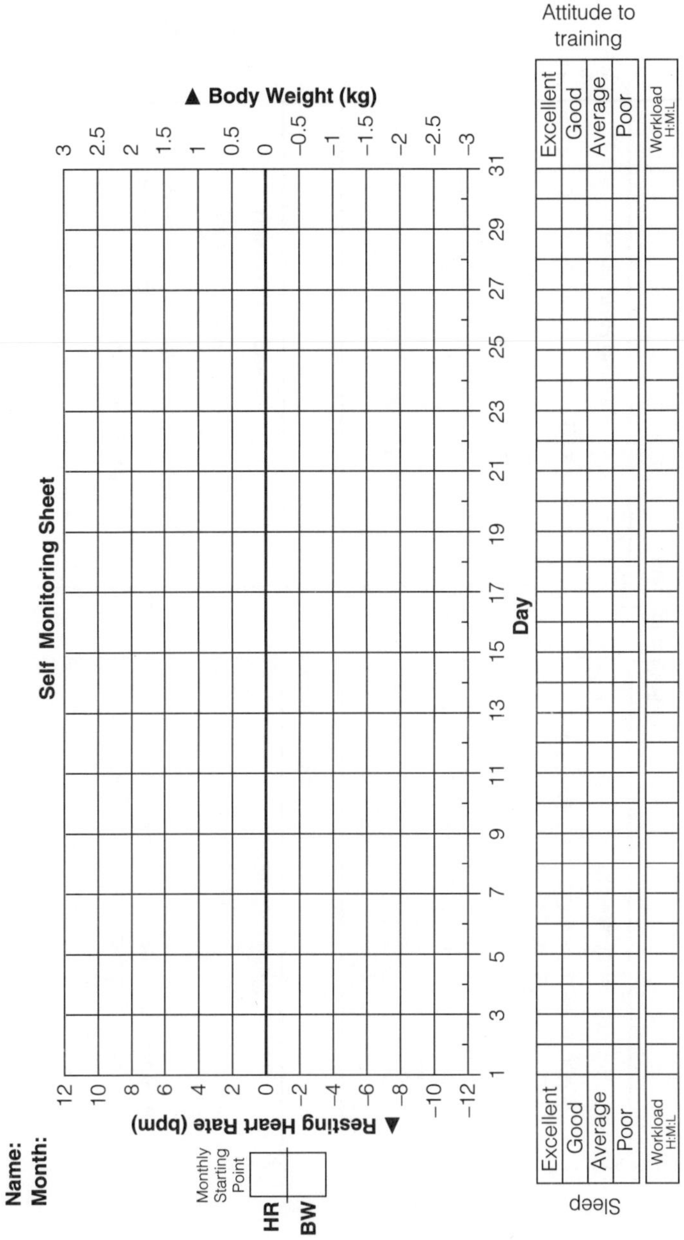

Name:
Month:

Self Monitoring Sheet

101

Figure 6.3: Self-monitoring sheet

Record Each Daily

Body Weight

- Record each morning before eating and after going to the toilet.
- Body weight is not a measure of fat stores, so
- Do not worry about small fluctuations in weight, but
- Unexplained weight loss may indicate overtraining

Resting Heart Rate

- Record RHR upon waking whilst still in bed

Recommended Scale

± 2 to 3 bpm above normal = OK to train
+ 5 bpm above normal = light training only
+ 10 bpm above normal = no training

Avoid Overtraining Problems

Sleep Patterns

- Record quality of sleep each night
- Minimum of 8 to 10 hours recommended

Regulate daily Biorhythms by

- Going to bed and getting up at the same times each day
- Keep to the same wake-up time even if you have a late night

Attitude to Training

- Record your feeling about training
- Feeling tired after training is normal *BUT* continuous fatigue (several days) = *poor recovery*
- If regularly tired, take a day off or try another and lighter activity

Table 6.2: An athlete's observations of non-adaptation

- sudden drop in body weight (more than 3%)
- sudden increase in morning heart rate of > 6 bpm
- inability to respond to relaxation or meditation techniques
- sleep disturbances (plus or minus 2 hours for more than 2 days)
- low quality sleep for more than 2 days
- feeling constantly tired

Source: Tim Frick (1993), Canadian wheelchair basketball coach.

knowing how valuable this information can be. The coach has to provide an alternative for the uninterested or stubborn athlete. A simple and quick self-assessment method is given in Table 6.3. The variables assessed can be changed to suit different circumstances but the outcome is essentially the same. How you feel is often the best indication of how you are coping.

Body-clocks and training adaptations

All mammals have body-clocks or biorhythms that can be manipulated by sleeping times, exposure to natural light, and meal times. Humans are diurnal, being most active in daylight and slowing down in the evening and at night. This daily variation alters the metabolic demands on the body, reflected by a fall of 1°C in core body temperature from midday to midnight. Going to bed with a falling core temperature and getting up in the morning as this temperature is rising is the normal behaviour pattern for humans. Late nights, sleeping in, irregular eating habits or travelling to different time zones (jet lag) can disrupt this natural pattern and lead to unnecessary fatigue in athletes. This extra fatigue can delay the adaptive processes, particularly if disruption to the biological clock is frequent, as it is with shift work. Shift workers have

Table 6.3: Self-assessment mood table (tick how you feel)

	Happy	Indifferent	Upset
Physically			
Psychologically			
Emotionally			

greater difficulty adapting to training loads as their disrupted biorhythms frequently leave them feeling tired.

However, this need for athletes to regulate their sleeping habits does not prevent them from having a social life and enjoying the occasional late night. To cope with late nights, athletes should be encouraged to standardise their wake-up time wherever possible. Sleeping in after a late night should be limited to one hour within the normal wake-up time, so there is minimal disruption to sleep patterns. Extra sleep can be gained through a short nap, no longer than one hour, preferably after lunch.

Similarly, the body adapts to meal times so it is important to plan for regular eating times. Although we have no shortage of natural light in Australia, some countries overseas have relatively small periods of natural light during winter months, which can affect an athlete's body-clock and mood states. Seasonal variations in Australia, unlike those in some northern European countries, are not so great as to require treatments to offset this occurrence.

Passive and active rest

Passive rest: Sleep is the most important form of passive rest. A good night's sleep of seven to nine hours provides invaluable adaptation time for athletes to adjust to the physical and emotional stressors they experience during the day. Other forms of passive rest involve techniques which help the mind to switch off from all the surrounding stimuli. Getting to sleep can sometimes be difficult because of the excitement of a day's events, so it is important to develop habits to promote a good night's sleep (Table 6.4).

Meditation, flotation, reading or listening to relaxing music are other forms of passive rest. Some of these are readily accessible to all athletes but a few are restrictive because they require special training or are quite expensive.

Table 6.4: How to develop good sleeping habits

Things to do
1. Practise relaxation techniques before going to bed (relaxing music, muscle relaxation, breathing exercises, visualisation).
2. Lie down to sleep *only* when you are sleepy.
3. If you don't fall asleep within 30 minutes after turning out the light get up and do some relaxation work (see point 1).
4. If you wake up in the night and can't go back to sleep follow point 3.
5. Get up at the same time each day.

Things to avoid in the evening
1. Caffeine (e.g. coffee, tea, cola drinks, chocolate)
2. Nicotine
3. Alcohol
4. High protein meals
5. Reduce thinking and worrying in bed—learn to switch off

Active rest is greatly undervalued by many athletes. The end of the loading component of the training session is an ideal time to introduce active recovery activities, although active rest can also be incorporated throughout the session. Active recoveries can fulfil two main tasks. They can either help recover an athlete's physiological state (e.g. light walking or cycling to recover the lactate system), or they can focus on musculoskeletal recovery (e.g. stretching and exercises to promote postural efficiency). Including both types of activities briefly at the end of a training session, especially after heavy speed or endurance training sessions, competition or a heavy training week, are simple ways to incorporate active recovery into training programs.

Cross training can often be used as a form of active rest, provided the work intensities are modest (light aerobic) and the exercises undertaken are different to those normally performed in training. Pool work, either walking or swimming, particularly backstroke and side stroke, are excellent modes of active recovery after a game or race and are now frequently used by many elite football teams and athletes.

Rest days are essential. At least one day per week should be a non-training day. This allows athletes time for physical recovery as well as time to develop interests outside their sport, so they can have a balanced lifestyle. The old truism, 'All work and no play makes Jack a dull boy', reflects the need for variety in order to prevent staleness and boredom.

An athlete with one or two interests beside sport can provide for this stimulation more readily than the athlete who focuses on sport to the exclusion of everything else. Finding the balance between study, training, and social and domestic commitments is one of the biggest challenges for most athletes. Rest days enable them to maintain a healthy balance in their lives.

Fluid and fuel for recovery

The planning required to prepare for an event or training session should include provision afterwards for the replenishment of fluid and fuel stores used during training. Athletes are responsible for balancing their nutritional intake in accordance with the demands of their training (see Chapter 8).

Replacing fluid and glycogen (carbohydrate) stores after training is important for most sports. Carbohydrate loading pre-event is designed to maximise the storage of glycogen and minimise the onset of fatigue. As metabolism is increased during and after exercise the optimal time for replenishing glycogen stores is within the first hour following exercise. The recommended intake is 1g of carbohydrate per kilogram of body weight per hour. It is especially important to eat carbohydrates following eccentric exercise, such as strength and speed sessions, or following heavy contact which has led to bruising. Muscle damage delays muscle glycogen rebuilding, particularly after the first 48 hours, therefore it is important to maximise the time when there is an increase in glycogen building by providing a high post-exercise carbohydrate intake during the following 24 hours.

Monitoring fluid loss can minimise the risks of dehydration. A body weight loss of 2% or more during exercise results in measurable physiological changes that can lead to a reduction in performance. Educating athletes to drink in order to keep pace with sweat rates is important; this can be monitored through urine checks (clear urine is ideal) and pre- and post-training weighing (1 kg lost = 1 litre of fluid). For an event lasting less than 60 minutes, water should suffice, but for longer events isotonic sports drinks (Gatorade,

---

Table 6.5: Fatigue-fighters checklist

After each training session

- Drink and eat
- Walk/move (at least 5 minutes)
- Stretch
- Hot/cold shower

Evening/end of day

- Hot/cold shower/spa/sauna
- Stretch and self massage (especially legs)
- Practise relaxation 10–15 minutes before bed (music, progressive muscle relaxation, visualisation, breathing exercises)

Note:

- Monitor how you feel each day.
- Get up at the same time each day.
- Record how you feel (i.e. great, tired, stuffed).
- You need at least four hours between training sessions.

Exceed, etc.) which help to stimulate the desire to drink and help to restore electrolyte balances and provide carbohydrate are recommended.

Minerals and trace elements such as zinc and magnesium are important for muscle regeneration after training. However, extra intake of these from synthetic supplements may not be as effective as extra intake from increased dietary sources, due to the reactivity of some elements and metals with other foodstuffs in the gut. Professional nutritional advice is recommended for those athletes who experience considerable muscle damage, or for those who are continually fatigued. Iron deficiencies or problems with absorption are not uncommon in male and female athletes. If an athlete is consistently tired, the above checklist may help to eliminate possible causes and point the athlete in the direction of appropriate professional help if fatigue persists (Table 6.5).

PHYSICAL THERAPIES

Hydrotherapies

A wide range of physical therapies which aid recovery is available to athletes. Hydrotherapies (water-based) and sports

---

Table 6.6: Guidelines for hydrotherapies

How to use
- Rehydrate before, during, and after session.
- Clean skin with soap and shower off beforehand.

Alternate: Hot (35–38°C)	Cold (10–16°C)
Shower 1–2 minutes	(10–30 seconds) repeat × 3
Or	
Spa/bath 3–4 minutes	(30–60 seconds) repeat × 3

- Shower and rehydrate to finish.

When to use
- Showers can be used any time—before, during or after a session.
- Spas and baths are best left till the end of the day (unless the athlete uses them properly, when they can be used earlier).

Note: An athlete who has a virus, a cold or a recent soft tissue injury should not use a spa.

---

massage are the two most frequently used. Showers, spas, baths, float tanks and saunas (dry baths), provide ideal environments in which to stretch and perform self-massage. The use of contrasting hot and cold showers, or a warm spa with a cold plunge pool, stimulates an increase in both peripheral (muscle/skin) circulation and neural (nervous system) stimulation. Pressure from jets and shower nozzles enhances muscle relaxation by stimulating light contractions in the muscles. All these water therapies promote both physiological and neurological recovery.

Athletes need to be reminded to rehydrate before, during, and after water treatments as sweating tends to go unnoticed in wet environments. It is also important that treatment times are carefully monitored (Table 6.6). Giving in to the temptation to linger in the warm environment will offset the benefits of the treatment through dehydration and nervous system fatigue. An athlete should feel relaxed but stimulated afterwards, not sleepy and lethargic.

Sports massage

The other frequently used recovery method is sports massage (refer to Table 6.7). Massage has two major physiological benefits. Firstly, it can increase blood flow which in turn enhances the delivery of oxygen and nutrients to tired muscles as well as promoting the removal of metabolic byproducts such as lactic acid. Secondly, the warming and

---

Table 6.7: Sports massage treatments

The five basic terms describing massage techniques are: vibration (shaking), tapotement (percussion), petrisage (kneading), effleurage (stroking) and friction (small range intensive stroking).

Sports massage using different combinations of these techniques is regarded as one of the most effective means of recovery. Treatments are administered during three phases of training:

Within training sessions: massage is given during training sessions to help accommodate high training loads and to increase the athlete's training potential.

Preparatory massage: as part of a warm-up* phase can be given 15–20 minutes before competition. Techniques can be varied so that the massage can either relax an overstimulated athlete or arouse an apathetic one. Sometimes the massage is localised to an injured area in an effort to prepare it before activity.

Restorative massage: is given in the post-loading part of a training session or competition. The techniques used aim to reduce muscle tension and fatigue and lower stress levels. The length and number of massage treatments varies depending on the type of activity (e.g. concentric or eccentric loading), the intensity of the activity and the state of the individual athlete. Elite performers need at least two full body massages per week.

Note: Massage is an adjunct only to a sport specific warm-up. It should never replace an active warm-up which prepares the body both physiologically and neurologically for specific sports activities.

---

stretching of soft tissues through massage provides temporary flexibility gains. There are also psychological benefits—as tired tight muscles relax there is a corresponding improvement in mood states. Athletes feel less fatigued and more relaxed.

Perhaps the greatest benefit from a sports massage is the biofeedback athletes gain as they become more aware of their bodies and which muscles and tendons are stressed. Tuning in to the way the body has been stressed helps an athlete identify and manage the stressed and fatigued areas.

Sports massage has gained wide acceptance over the past ten years. There are now many well qualified professionals available. If an athlete finds the cost of professional massage prohibitive, self-massage techniques are free and easy to administer, particularly for the lower legs, chest, neck, shoulders and forearms. Lower leg massages in particular are an effective way to minimise compartment problems such as shin splints, or repetitive strain problems. Self-massage techniques take only a few minutes to perform; they are best done in a relaxing atmosphere (e.g. while watching television or in the shower or bath).

Acupuncture and acupressure

Acupressure is often used as an adjunct to sports massage. Acupuncture requires more extensive qualifications and consequently is less accessible and more expensive. Both techniques focus on balancing energy fields via specific points located on fourteen meridians which pass through the body. Acupuncture points have a lower cutaneous electrical resistance than adjacent areas (these can be measured and evaluated). Stimulation of specific points is claimed to influence a wide variety of body functions, including oxygen uptake, respiration and the immune system.

Unfortunately, few reliable scientific studies have been conducted, although a recent reputable study from China has demonstrated that muscles relax more after acupuncture than without the treatment.

Hyperbaric oxygenation therapy

Hyperbaric oxygenation therapy (HBO) is a means of increasing the availability of oxygen to the body, achieved by inhaling gas with a high oxygen content in an environment with increased atmospheric pressure. The most common technique is to present the client (patient/athlete) with 100% oxygen at two atmospheres of pressure. This increases the partial pressure of oxygen in the body, which means that oxygen molecules can reach damaged and fatigued body parts more easily than under normal atmospheric pressures and conditions where oxygen content is about 21%. The technology has only recently been applied to sporting situations in Australia and it has focused on accelerating the repair process for injuries. In the former Soviet Union, HBO has also been used to accelerate training adaptations, particularly in athletes undertaking anaerobic training activities. HBO is still in its infancy in Australia and is unlikely to be readily available to many athletes. There is some controversy amongst medical specialists about the effectiveness of HBO as an aid to injury repair, and its effectiveness in accelerating adaptation to training awaits further research.

PSYCHOLOGICAL SKILLS (PSYCHO-REGULATORY TRAINING)

Developing the ability to control emotions and mood states through the application of a few simple psychological skills is as beneficial to an athlete as to any other person. In particular, improving self awareness and motivation, and decreasing reactions to stress, are essential life skills. Recognition of the complex interaction and strong relationship between physical and mental states is important for recovery training. This can be demonstrated when muscle relaxation is complemented by lowered heart rates and blood pressure and by improved mood states. The term used to refer to the techniques and skills employed to aid an athlete's emotional and psychological state in this way is 'psycho-regulatory training (PRT)'. Relaxation techniques, meditation, autogenic training, breathing exercises, music, relaxation massage and flotation are the most frequently used techniques.

Meditation

Although passive rest is an important component of recovery practices, the time spent during passive rest can be used to include one of several PRT techniques. Meditation trains the athlete to relax by controlling the parasympathetic (calming) nervous system through reducing 'noise' (stimulation) to the brain. By controlling this system the athlete can lower blood pressure and heart rate, slow down breathing rates, relax muscles and calm the sympathetic (excitatory) nervous system. This technique is useful for controlling stresses from training or competition, particularly if the athlete is over-aroused. Meditation skills take some time and plenty of practice to acquire and they are most readily learned by young athletes.

Progressive muscle relaxation

Progressive muscle relaxation (PMR) can be done at the end of training or before going to bed. The technique involves tightening and relaxing specific muscle groups so that the athlete identifies the sensations of muscle tension and muscle relaxation in that body part. This reduces muscle tension and helps to improve body awareness so the athlete can more readily recognise muscle tension and focus on reducing it. When this skill is used regularly in training it can significantly improve the quality of training and the athlete's competitive abilities.

Autogenic training

Autogenic training is similar to PMR. This is a self-induction technique which requires the athlete to focus on producing sensations in specific muscle groups. The two sensations most commonly used to promote relaxation are warmth and heaviness. Warm sensations, which indicate a relaxed state, provide a useful focus for many athletes after stressful situations.

Imagery and visualisation

All athletes have a sense of imagination which can be developed to contribute to their training potential. Imagery relaxation and visualisation involve using the imagination to create a vivid scene. The four senses of sight, smell, sound, and touch can be used together to generate an image which should evoke feelings of comfort and relaxation.

Breathing

Breathing exercises are used frequently in the martial arts, a recognition of the fact that learning breathing techniques and focusing on relaxing tense muscles leads to a more relaxed state. Exhaling while applying static stretches also helps produce a relaxation response in the body.

REST and flotation

Another group of psychological relaxation techniques revolves around the concept of REST (restricted environment stimulation therapy). Some skills are as simple as closing the eyes to reduce stimulation while other techniques require training (meditation) or specialised equipment (flotation). Reducing the amount of stimulation to the brain enables the athlete to focus more effectively on relaxing and becoming emotionally calm.

Flotation tanks provide an environment with minimal stimulation by reproducing weightlessness and eliminating the stimulation of both sight and sound (unless the athlete relaxes to music or to an affirmation tape). Most people need two or three trials to learn how to relax completely using a flotation tank, but it is remarkably effective for reducing stress and preventing burnout—particularly in over-stressed coaches!

Music

Music as an adjunct to training is under-utilised. Although it is sometimes used in the weights gym to provide motivation for hard work, it is equally effective in evoking a relaxation response if the appropriate music is selected. Most athletes have access to a Walkman or tape deck so they can create a bank of tapes to generate a range of atmospheres, from stimulating to calming. Tapes can be used in training, and because they are quite portable are an excellent tool in competition or when an athlete is having difficulty relaxing in an unfamiliar environment. With practice an athlete can learn to manipulate mood states for optimal arousal or relaxation.

Apart from flotation, which requires specialised facilities, and music, which requires a tape player, all these psycho-regulatory techniques can be practised daily in any quiet place. An ideal time is immediately before going to bed. Learning how to switch off from the day's events will also promote a good night's sleep.

Emotional recovery

At key times during the year, such as competitions and tournaments, school or university exams and Christmas, athletes are often excessively stressed. If they have lost a game or competition, or performed below their expectations, they may benefit from some emotional recovery work in their training program. Mood-lifting activities can include watching an amusing video or a comedy show, reading an escapist or adventure novel, or going to a fun park, zoo or light entertainment centre. For teams or athletes in extended competitions, planning such activities as part of training can be most beneficial.

PUTTING IT ALL TOGETHER: PERIODISING RECOVERY TRAINING

Off season/transition/early preparatory phase

The transition training phase is the most important period for developing the techniques of recovery training. Just as pre-season screening is essential to detect any potential problems which may be exacerbated by training during the season, so this is the time when athletes should start their self-monitoring programs and learn to tune in to their bodies. Some of the most essential recovery techniques should be introduced and reinforced during this phase. These include appropriate nutrition, stretching (including postural efficiency exercises), hydrotherapies, self massage and one or two of the relaxation techniques discussed above.

Specific preparatory/conditioning/pre-competitive phase

The specific preparatory phase is an ideal time to introduce planning skills. Athletes need to know how to balance their training sessions in relation to their other priorities such as work or study, and their home and social lives. Self-monitoring should become a habit, regularly reinforced by the coach. The increase in training loads during this phase leads to an increase in musculoskeletal stress. This in turn increases the need for more physical recovery techniques, especially nutrition, hydrotherapies, massage, active recovery activities, cross training and postural correction techniques. Reinforcing and extending knowledge and availability of these techniques is essential.

Psychological skills which promote muscle relaxation are also important. Athletes should practise the relaxation techniques they plan to use during competition and put together a bank of appropriate music to use in their training for relaxation.

Competition phase

By the time the competition phase arrives all recovery skills should be automatic. Athletes should be familiar with self-recording and self-management strategies. They should know how and when to use all the techniques they have practised and be comfortable using them during intense competition. There may be a heavier reliance on psychological recovery during this phase because of the stress of competition. However, if the competition program is planned in advance and athletes know and understand their requirements, their stress levels will be lower and they will have more control over their physical and psychological states. Coaches need to plan carefully to include appropriate recovery training activities around competition demands in order to maximise recovery from one game or event to the next. This includes planning time out and entertainment so that there is a suitable balance between stress and relaxation.

RESPONSIBILITIES FOR RECOVERY TRAINING

At the beginning of the training year coaches and athletes should arrive at a clear understanding of their distinct but complementary responsibilities for recovery training, and both should agree to undertake these respective responsibilities.

This agreement can be in the form of an unwritten contract or 'gentleman's agreement', but it is essential that both coach and athlete have a clear understanding of their respective roles and duties for recovery training.

The coach and recovery training

The overall planning of workloads and the appropriate rest ratios is the responsibility of the coach. To assess adaptation to training loads the coach needs to monitor each athlete for any signs or symptoms of non-adaptation on a regular basis (refer to Table 6.2). To encourage appropriate levels of adaptation the coach must familiarise athletes with the necessary self-monitoring techniques and self-management skills. A wise coach will also recognise the external demands placed on athletes, such as exams or work, and tailor training loads to complement these external pressures so that the athletes do not become excessively stressed.

Coaches must recognise that not many of them will have all the knowledge or skills required to teach recovery activities, so they should be prepared to use other specialists to educate athletes about management strategies such as self massage. Every coach, however, has the responsibility of reinforcing this educational aspect of the training program by encouraging and reviewing the application of recovery techniques and activities regularly.

Training programs need to be flexible so that coaches have the option of changing workloads in response to the adaptive responses of individual athletes. This flexibility must also apply to the different requirements placed on athletes by different environments and venues.

The athlete and recovery training

Athletes have two major responsibilities. Firstly, they need to learn to listen to their bodies; and secondly, they need to look after themselves physically and psychologically. The very least an athlete can do to fulfil these responsibilities is outlined in Table 6.8.

Table 6.8: Athlete's responsibilities for recovery training

Monitoring and management strategies

Daily
- Every morning monitor resting heart rate, body weight, and quality of sleep.
- Each evening, rate fatigue/tiredness for the day.
- Eat a balanced diet and plan meals and snacks to complement training.
- Use shower/spa/bath for stretching, self massage, and hot and cold contrasts.
- Before bed practise a relaxation technique (e.g. music, visualisation, PMR, breathing exercises).

Weekly
- Have at least one rest day.
- Plan active rest (e.g. stretching, postural exercises, cross training).
- Organise a massage (commercial, partner or parent) and use self massage at least three times.

Weekly time management (plan in advance)
- Prioritise all weekly commitments (work, study, training, domestic, social events).

If athletes learn the essential skills of self-monitoring and self-management not only will they optimise their chances of adapting to heavy workloads, but they will also be developing effective life skills which they can use after they have finished their competitive careers.

CONCLUSION

Intense pressure on athletes and coaches to improve results has increased the necessity to train hard, but sometimes this is achieved at too high a cost. Athletes and coaches often fall victim to illnesses associated with excessive stress, and the temptation to train harder in order to succeed becomes very attractive. Finding a balance in a training program so that best performances can be realised without the athlete or coach breaking down has often been difficult because many coaches and athletes have been unaware of the role and benefits of recovery training.

The principle of recovery is the most frequently forgotten training component and the most poorly understood of all the training principles. Yet recovery training is as important for an athlete's development as are the improvement of energy systems, strength and flexibility and the training of

117

mental skills. The many benefits to athletes of integrating recovery training effectively within training programs include:

- Learning how to monitor their training responses and manage themselves so they can cope with their workloads and stresses
- Reducing the incidence of injuries, illnesses and burnout often experienced by overstressed athletes and coaches is a spin-off from successful adaptation
- Safe and natural alternatives to banned performance-enhancing drugs
- The acquisition of effective life skills in self-awareness, self-management, and self-maintenance which athletes and coaches can use even after they have finished their competitive sporting careers.

Recovery activities offer a great deal of scope for designing training regimens specific to the physiological and psychological needs of individual athletes. Responsibility for monitoring adaptation and implementing recovery training is a shared responsibility between the coach and athlete. If both are committed to working hard and adapting well they can achieve their best performance.

SUMMARY

- Recovery training is as important as hard training in optimising sports performance.
- An astute coach should be looking for the signs and symptoms of an athlete failing to adapt to training. An astute athlete should monitor these factors on a daily basis. These factors include tiredness, poor technique, increased resting heart rate, loss of body weight, loss of appetite, low motivation, aggressiveness and poor sleeping habits.

- Athletes and coaches should ensure recovery is enhanced through passive rest (sleep, reading), active recovery (light workouts, cross training), correct nutritional practices, physical therapies (hydrotherapies, massage, acupuncture and acupressure) and psychological skills training (meditation, relaxation, flotation, music).
- Recovery training should be periodised. Recovery techniques should be developed during the off-season and transition phases of training, and become automatic during the competition phase.
- Recovery training is a shared responsibility between the coach and the athlete.

RECOMMENDED READING

Burke, L. (1995) *The Complete Guide to Food for Sports Performance*, 2nd edn, Allen & Unwin, Sydney.

Calder, A. (1992) *Recovery Planner*, available from the Australian Coaching Council, PO Box 176, Belconnen ACT 2616 (a useful planning tool for recovery training).

Clews, W. (1990) *Sports Massage and Stretching*, Bantam Books, Sydney.

Rushall, B.S. and F.S. Pyke (1990) *Training for Sport and Fitness*, Macmillan Australia, available from The Australian Coaching Council, PO Box 176, Belconnen, ACT 2616.

Video

Calder, A. (1992) *Planning and Recovery*, from *Beyond Barcelona, 4th Elite Coaches Seminar*, available from the Australian Coaching Council, PO Box 176, Belconnen, ACT 2616.

7

Injury treatment and prevention

Michael Dalgleish and Matthew Freke

Injury is the bane of every athlete, whether the Sunday jogger or the elite athlete competing on the international stage. Not only are injuries painful and frustrating but they can be costly both in terms of treatment and of lost earnings through time off work or away from professional sport. The most effective treatment of injuries is, therefore, prevention. This chapter begins by outlining strategies of prevention, and then reviews the basic principles of injury management.

Most injuries can be prevented if the body is prepared for the exercise to be undertaken. In the long term, this means specific training for a particular sport. Most athletes can probably remember a time when they participated in an unfamiliar sport and how sore they felt afterwards. This soreness arises from using unfamiliar muscles in unfamiliar patterns of movement. Acquiring the physical condition needed to decrease soreness and reduce the possibility of injury may be considered as acquiring the five 'S's—strength, speed, skill, suppleness and stamina.

- Strength is the ability of muscle to exert a force against resistance. A degree of strength is important in all sports, not only for force development but injury prevention.
- Speed is the ability to make successive movements in

the shortest possible time, or the ability to move quickly. This may involve the whole body, or just parts of the body.

- Skill is described as a special ability or expertise, often acquired by training. The most skilful way of performing an activity is often the most biomechanically correct way. Thus, the greater the skill, the less chance of injury.
- Suppleness is the extensibility of muscle, joint capsule, ligament, tendon and nerve. Suppleness or flexibility is important in most sports. A good range of joint movement is necessary for ease and freedom of movement.
- Stamina or endurance is the ability of the individual to maintain continued large muscle group contractions over an extended period of time. Muscular fatigue is related to injury; it follows that the less stamina, the earlier the fatigue, and the earlier the possibility of injury.

The development of speed and stamina is discussed in other chapters within this book. Suppleness will be examined in detail shortly.

PREVENTION OF INJURY

Prevention of injury, largely achieved through warm-up, warm-down and a good level of fitness, is better than cure. Other considerations in the bid to prevent injury include:

- Developing skills and technique specific to your sport—studies show the higher the level of skill the lower the rate of injury.
- Obeying the rules—many rules in sport are designed to make the game safer for all concerned. Coaches should develop a respect for the codes of the game.
- Using well-maintained playing areas and facilities—inadequate playing surfaces, poorly designed or faulty equipment may place the athletes and the public at risk. It is important that playing areas are level and firm, free from obstructions and that spectators have a safe area away from the playing area.

- Using protective devices—many sports injuries can be prevented by wearing the appropriate braces or padding (e.g. mouth guards, shin guards, helmets).
- Adjusting for environmental conditions—during summer months, sunburn can be a major problem, so athletes should remember to cover up and use their SPF15+. Fluid replacement is also important. During winter months, cold weather can cause problems by reducing body temperature quickly. Long breaks in activity should be avoided and adequate clothing (e.g. tracksuits for warm-up) should be worn.
- Responding sensibly to illness or medical conditions—it is not advisable for an athlete to participate in any sporting activity while sick. If you have doubts about competing while unwell consult a sports physician first.

WARM-UP

In the short term, the body can be prepared for strenuous activity by warming-up. Warm-ups can be broken down into four phases:

General warm-up

General warm-ups, through active movements of the major muscle groups in activities such as easy jogging, swimming and cycling, are the most widely used techniques to increase the overall body temperature. The aim is to raise the core temperature of the body by 1–2°C, thereby making the muscles, ligaments and tendons more compliant to stretch. Other benefits of warm-up include increased muscle cell metabolism; a decrease in the viscosity of synovial fluid (the fluid that provides lubrication of the joints) which makes movement of the joints easier; increased blood and oxygen supply to working muscle; elevated body temperature, making it easier for the muscle to pick up oxygen from the blood; and increased sensitivity and speed of nerve conduction.

The warm-up should be easy to begin with and gradually increase in intensity. The most obvious indicator of a successful general warm-up is a light sweat. This phase of the warm-up should take five to ten minutes and is mandatory to gain maximum effect out of the phases that follow. Because the body of a well-conditioned athlete is capable of responding more efficiently to heat produced during exercise, athletes at peak conditioning may require longer or more intensive warm-ups than less well-conditioned athletes, particularly in colder weather.

Stretching

The second phase of an adequate warm-up to prevent injury is stretching, using a specific program of stretches designed for the particular sport. Improving flexibility through stretching is an important preparatory activity for enhanced physical performance. Lack of flexibility may result in uncoordinated or awkward movements and may predispose an individual to muscle strain. Some sports, such as gymnastics or karate, require more flexibility than others. There are two main types of stretch to be used in a warm-up, ballistic and static.

Static stretching involves passively stretching a muscle to the point of discomfort and holding it there for an extended period. The time of hold has been much debated, expert opinions ranging from 3 to 60 seconds. Since a stretch of longer than 6 seconds is needed to overcome the natural resistance to stretch and allow the muscle to relax, it seems logical that 6 seconds should be considered the minimum hold time.

Ballistic stretching makes use of repetitive bouncing motions. Although this type of stretching is specific to many sporting activities it should be used with care as it can be associated with over-stretch and injury. It is safest to carry out ballistic stretching after more gentle static stretching has already lengthened the muscle. The intensity should be slowly increased and its introduction to a program should be graduated.

Stretches can be further divided into three other categories: muscle, nerve and joint stretches.

Muscle stretches are the most commonly performed stretches. Follow these simple rules:

- Always do a general warm-up prior to stretching, to make the muscles more elastic and easier to stretch.
- Stretch before and after exercise.
- Stretch to the point of discomfort, not pain.
- Try and breathe normally while stretching.
- Never bounce or stretch rapidly unless you are certain you are able to achieve the range of movement aimed for.
- Hold static stretches for at least six seconds.
- Stretch each muscle group three or four times.
- Technique is important—always stretch in straight lines and avoid excessive rotation of the limb being stretched. Rotation changes the emphasis of the stretch, meaning some parts of the muscle get a lot of stretch while other parts get very little. Sometimes this emphasis is desirable, sometimes it isn't. If in doubt, stay straight.
- Consider: Are you stretching what you want to stretch? The body will move along lines of least resistance during stretch, so stretching of a tight muscle should be felt in that muscle (normally in the muscle belly, not at its insertion), not elsewhere.
- Find out your tight areas and do extra work there. Examination by a physiotherapist will help determine which muscles or joints most need stretching.

Nerve stretches, which enhance mobilisation of the nervous system, are often ignored. When the body moves, the nerves that provide the power to the muscles have to move as well. They are not elastic, like muscle, but more like electrical wires. They glide through moving muscle and slide around moving joints. 'Nerve stretches' don't actually stretch nerves, but are an attempt to improve their movement by improving their ability to slide and glide. Here are some simple rules to follow with nerve stretches:

- Movement, rather than stretch, is the important consideration in nerve mobilisation.
- The movement used in nerve mobilisation should be kept within pain-free limits.
- Each mobilisation should be repeated ten times.

For examples of nerve stretches, see *Sport Stretch* in 'Recommended reading'.

Joint stretches: Many of the stretches prescribed for muscles also put the underlying joints through a good range of movement but specific stretching, or mobilisation, of joints helps the warm-up procedure. All joints are surrounded by a joint capsule which helps control the joint movement and holds in the joint's lubricating fluid. In the capsule and surrounding ligaments are nerve endings which give feedback (proprioception) on joint position. The brain's awareness of a joint can be increased by stimulating these nerve endings, most easily done by putting the joint through a range of movement that increases tension in the joint capsule. The book *Sport Stretch* provides excellent examples of joint stretches useful for both speed and endurance athletes. Importantly, the sequencing and techniques for individual stretches should be implemented and supervised by trained professionals such as sports physiotherapists.

Specific warm-up

After completing a general warm-up consisting of easy exercise and stretching, the athlete should progress to exercise that is specific for a particular event or activity. Any exercise which involves movements similar to the actual athletic event, but at a reduced level of intensity, is classified as a specific warm-up. For example, a distance runner would warm up for an event by performing light-to-moderate running, a swimmer may swim at a reduced level in the practice pool. In a sport like Rugby League the player may practise up and back, or side to side, running. A specific warm-up not only increases the temperature of the body parts directly involved in the activity, but also provides a rehearsal of the event to take place.

Specific warm-up should begin at a moderate pace and increase in tempo as the body temperature and cardiovascular changes take place. The effects of warm-up may last as long as 45 minutes, but the closer the warm-up is to the activity, the better. Ideally no more than 15 minutes should elapse between completion of warm-up and performance of activity.

Finally, the specific warm-up should be aimed at the athlete's particular fitness level. Too long or strenuous a warm-up may tire an athlete and impair subsequent performance.

Practising skills

Practice of specific skills for the sport should be the final component of warm-up, once the musculoskeletal system of the body is warmed up and ready to perform. Within team sports each team member may have specific tasks to prepare for. For example, a soccer goal-keeper requires different skills to a mid-fielder so these should be practised separately. The skills practice should be at the same tempo as a game situation.

WARM-DOWNS

The warm-down is just as important as the warm-up. During exercise the body often accumulates end-products such as lactic acid. After intense exercise, especially in speed sports, these end-products can slow recovery. An important reason for warming-down is that blood and muscle lactic acid levels decrease more rapidly during active recovery than during passive recovery. Also, active recovery keeps the muscles pumping, which prevents blood pooling in the arms and legs. Warm-downs are especially important if the athlete intends to compete again in a short period of time, e.g. 24 hours.

The warm-down generally consists of two stages, a general warm-down and stretching.

General warm-down

General warm-down is similar to general warm-up, although the intensity is reduced. It should consist of approximately five to ten minutes of mild aerobic activity, e.g. jogging, to promote circulation of blood through the muscles used so that end-products can be removed.

Stretching

The same stretches used in the warm-up should be used, with special consideration shown to tight or sore muscle groups. Athletes who stretch after activity tend to have fewer problems with muscle soreness and stiffness, which can result from lack of blood flow to the working tissues.

Other recovery strategies such as fluid and energy replacement and massage after activity are discussed in other chapters.

INJURY MANAGEMENT

Even though every effort is made to prevent them, injuries will still occur. The risk of injury is an inherent part of most speed and endurance sports. Everyone involved in sport has a responsibility to manage that risk and keep it to a minimum. They also have a responsibility to manage appropriately the injuries that do occur under their supervision. The golden rule in managing injury is:

DO NO FURTHER DAMAGE

Inadequate first aid may aggravate the injury and cause an increase in the time needed for recuperation before returning to play. Either the coach or some other official involved with the sport should have some training in basic injury assessment and management.

INJURY ASSESSMENT

It is important to have an organised approach to assessing injury. This gives confidence to the injured athlete and reduces the chances of misdiagnosing and the risk of aggravating the injury. Following basic guidelines helps achieve all of these aims. Remember: if you think the injury is more serious than you are able to deal with—**get help!** For more information on injury management, attend the excellent courses run by sports medicine organisations that cater to all levels of on-field management of sporting teams.

Two vitally important mnemonics, illustrated in Tables 7.1 and 7.2, will help you to assess the injured athlete. They are DRABC and STOP.

Table 7.1: DRABC

- **D = Danger**
  Always check for possible danger to yourself, the injured athlete and others. This may mean getting the referee to halt the game or removing the athlete from the field of play.
- **R = Response**
  Determine whether the athlete can respond to simple questioning. In many cases this may be obvious but when the athlete appears not to be with it you should attempt to get an appropriate response to simple questions.
  Examples: Can you hear me? What is your name? Can you open your eyes?
  If there is no response, send for an ambulance and/or qualified first aid support. Then check:
- **A = Airways**
  Check the athlete's mouth for obstructions to breathing. If necessary, open and clear the airways by removing possible obstructions such as teeth, vomitus, mouthguard or blood.
- **B = Breathing**
  If the athlete is not breathing, commence expired air resuscitation (EAR). If breathing, carefully place the athlete in the recovery position and await the ambulance.
- **C = Circulation**
  If there is no pulse, commence cardiopulmonary resuscitation (CPR). If a pulse is present and the athlete is breathing, carefully place in the recovery position and await the ambulance.
  If there is a response, begin assessment.

If the injured athlete responds to DRABC, move on to STOP, the second stage of assessment (Table 7.2).

Table 7.2: STOP

- **S = Stop**

  During initial assessment, you should stop the athlete from participating or moving. If necessary, you should stop the game by drawing the referee's attention to the problem.

- **T = Talk**

  This is the subjective examination of the athlete. From the sideline, it is not always possible to see exactly how the injury occurred. Even if you think you have a clear idea, you should always perform a subjective examination. The following questions are useful to help you determine the cause and nature of the injury.

  What happened?

  How did it happen?

  Did you hear anything?

  Where does it hurt?

  Does it hurt anywhere else?

  Have you injured this area before?

  You should use this initial contact with the athlete to offer a few words of encouragement. If it is a first contact situation and the athlete is not familiar to you, this time also fosters rapport and builds trust.

- **O = Observe**

  Observe the injured part while talking to the athlete. General observation:

  Is the athlete distressed?

  Is the athlete lying in an unusual position/posture?

  Injury site observation:

  Is there swelling? Immediate swelling is a sign of bleeding in the injury site and should be considered serious.

  Is there a difference when compared to the other side/limb?

  Is there tenderness when touched?

  Can the athlete move the injured part? If yes, does it hurt to move? Is the range restricted? Is the athlete able to functionally continue exercising? Tests for movement should progress from simple activities (e.g. movement of the part in lying or sitting position) to include more difficult tasks that are sport-specific (e.g. can the athlete jog on the spot).

- **P = Prevent further injury**

  Options vary depending on the severity of the injury.

  Severe injury, e.g. fractures, head or spinal injuries, major bleeding, facial injuries. Get professional help and don't move the athlete. Keep onlookers away and comfort the athlete until professional help arrives.

  Less severe injury, e.g. sprains, strains, bruises. Stop athlete from continuing with the game. Apply the PRICED regime, outlined in Table 7.3. Ensure the athlete gets follow-up medical care and advice if necessary (e.g. physiotherapy).

  Minor injury, e.g. bumps and bruises that do not impair performance. Allow the athlete to continue but monitor performance in the time following the injury to ensure that performance is not affected. Minor injuries can be treated with PRICED (see Table 7.3) after the game.

TREATMENT

The healing time of soft tissue injuries is greatly affected by the first aid action taken in the first 6 to 48 hours following injury. Time spent on the sideline recovering from injury can be reduced by following a few simple principles as soon as the injury occurs. When injury causes damage to muscle, tendon or ligament tissue, the process of healing begins immediately, following three general phases.

Phase one: inflammation

Immediately after injury occurs, blood and tissue fluids accumulate in the injured area. Rapid swelling denotes heavy bleeding, while slower swelling is produced by increased blood flow to the area and leakage from the damaged cells. The blood and tissue fluids collect to produce a clot (haematoma). Within the clot, tissue starts to form into a structure that becomes the starting point for repair. The inflammatory phase lasts up to 72 hours and is characterised by redness, heat, swelling, pain, and loss of function of the area. Managing this phase well is the key to minimising recovery time. Mobilisation, or excessive movement, during this stage may recommence the inflammatory reaction. An athlete should carry out the PRICED regime (discussed below) during this phase.

Table 7.3: PRICED

- **P = Prevention**
  The best management of all injuries is to prevent them! Strategies for prevention were discussed earlier in this chapter.
- **R = Rest**
  Rest reduces bleeding. Activity will promote bleeding by increasing blood flow, making the resultant clot larger and slower to heal. Place the athlete in a comfortable position, preferably lying down. The injured part should be immobilised and supported.
- **I = Ice**
  Application of ice reduces local circulation by decreasing the diameter of the blood vessels entering the area. Ice also reduces pain, swelling and muscle spasm. The conventional methods are: applying crushed ice in a wet towel/plastic bag, immersing the injured part in icy water, or applying commercial cold packs wrapped in a towel. Apply for approximately 20 minutes every 2 hours for the first 48 hours. *Caution*: do not apply ice directly to skin as ice burns may occur; do not apply ice to people who are sensitive to cold or have circulatory problems; note that children have a lower tolerance to ice.

- **C = Compression**
  Compression reduces bleeding and swelling by increasing pressure in the area and making local blood flow more difficult. Compression also provides support for the injured part. Apply a firm wide compression bandage over a large area covering the injured part, as well as above and below it. Always check the circulation below the bandaged area.
- **E = Elevation**
  Elevation reduces bleeding and swelling by using gravity. Fluid generally runs down-hill so if the injured part is elevated above heart level, less blood will be pumped up, and the swelling will drain away more easily. Elevation also reduces pain by decreasing pressure in the area. Raise the area above the level of the heart at all possible times.
- **D = Diagnosis**
  If you are concerned about the severity of the injury, or the athlete is still unable to train or play after the acute inflammation phase has passed, consult a sports medicine specialist.

Phase two: repair

The repair period can last up to 6 weeks, during which time processes take place within the damaged tissue that gradually remove the haematoma and replace it with fibrous scar tissue. The smaller the clot, the faster this healing process can proceed. The new scar tissue is not as organised or strong as the original undamaged tissue, so therapy to aid re-organisation of the fibres is necessary. Functional stress in the form of pain-free exercise during the repair phase will help lay down a stronger and more functional scar. A sports physician or physiotherapist should monitor this progressive pain-free exercise. Monitoring by professionals willl help produce a stronger and more functional scar.

Phase three: remodelling

The remodelling phase changes the unorganised scar tissue into a more ordered, parallel arrangement. The re-alignment of the new tissue fibres is helped by gradual activity, particularly stretching, and increasing intensity of exercise. The final outcome of successful remodelling is a stronger, longer replacement tissue which allows full normal movement. Phases two and three are not completely separate. During these stages the athlete is gradually returned to full activity but should be guided by sports medicine specialists such as sports physiotherapists or sports physicians.

The mnemonic PRICED, outlined in Table 7.3, is useful for remembering how to manage soft tissue injuries.

There are several things that should be avoided after injury, especially in the inflammatory phase:

- Heat—increases bleeding by increasing local circulation.
- Alcohol—increases swelling and bleeding by increasing the diameter of peripheral blood vessels.
- Exercise—running or exercising too soon can cause increased bleeding and break down fragile scar tissue.
- Massage—in the first 48–72 hours increases swelling and bleeding.

In summary, remember, when approaching an injured athlete, think: DRABC and STOP. In the treatment of an injured athlete, think: PRICED.

COMMON SPEED/ENDURANCE INJURIES

Hamstring tears

Management Tears of the hamstring group usually occur in the middle of the muscle belly or mid back of thigh. They are acute in onset and cause cessation of activity immediately. Symptoms other than these should be viewed with suspicion and referred to your sports physiotherapist or sports physician for accurate diagnosis. Early implementation of the PRICED regime is mandatory. The attainment of a full range of motion, i.e. no pain with straight leg raise, is a requirement prior to return to normal training. Normal range of motion in combination with appropriate strength and completion of activities over the total spectrum of functional movements required in the sport will indicate readiness to resume competition. Of course, the athlete should be symptom free with all training drills.

Prevention A strong relationship exists between repeated hamstring strain and the likelihood of a hidden back problem. Suspicion should be further heightened in the case of the adolescent athlete. A quality program of stretching should be implemented. Sequential involvement of the muscles of the back/hip/gluteals/hamstring group, followed by lower-back joints and, finally, gentle bouncing nerve stretches, will greatly reduce the incidence of injury and may alert athletes to areas where they are predisposed to injury. The hamstring has two primary functions in running: to decelerate the leg during swing (lengthening or eccentric contraction) and to aid the gluteals in extending the hip in stance (shortening or concentric contraction). Depending on the injury, prevention will aim to improve that type of contraction. Rehabilitation involves early work with the physiotherapist and later, working with a strength and conditioning specialist. Further prevention may be possible by functional assessment with elite physiological testing, e.g. isokinetic/eccentric assessment with Kincom/Cybex, functional assessment with the Plyopower, the less elaborate agility tests or vertical hop/side-ways hop. A comparison of a number of these tests may increase the reliability of prediction of predisposition.

Achilles tendonitis

Management With endurance training, athletes will often complain of pain in the achilles tendon or its sheath (external covering). Symptoms from the posterior ankle structures may be misdiagnosed as achilles tendonitis. The onset of pain is usually gradual but may be associated with rapid changes in intensity, frequency or duration of training or to a change of footwear. This injury falls into the overuse category, often in the presence of anatomical (anatomy) or faulty technique (biomechanics). It is unlikely that modification of training alone will alleviate symptoms on a permanent basis. Accurate diagnosis is always the key to effective management with all musculoskeletal pain. This may involve ultrasound to scan the injury and assess the degree of specific tendon involvement. Intervention early in the inflammation and pain cycle with appropriate stretching, PRICED, and if necessary, anti-inflammatory medication has proven useful. A regime of ankle and foot taping or orthosis (from the podiatrist) may also aid in early resolution of the problem. Minimal training will be lost if management is instituted early and effectively. Any quality stretching program will aim to correct those inflexibilities which are predisposing the athlete toward injury. This program may also include exercises to encourage better use of previously under-used muscles, thus improving technique.

Prevention A full assessment of the length and strength of the musculature of the pelvis, hip and leg is often necessary. The muscles of particular importance are the hip flexors, the gluteals, the quadriceps and the hamstrings. The specific components of the calf and achilles complex require assessment because of their direct influence on symptoms. The presence of abnormal foot structure may change the amount of torsion (or wringing) of the achilles tendon, which could predispose the athlete to injury. Video assessment may be reviewed by the coach, sports physiotherapist and sports podiatrist, and if required, serial taping or orthotic treatment may be instituted. A quality therapeutic program of stretching, self massage and muscular control exercises should result from this assessment. Drills to improve running and jumping techniques should be commenced and integrated into the athlete's periodisation. Not only will these changes alleviate the problem but they may also improve overall performance.

Shin splints

Management The term 'shin splints' is a lay term that describes any lower leg pain in a runner or an athlete engaged in a running sport. The condition commonly affects muscle, the places the muscle inserts onto bone, and the bone itself. Onset of shin splints is usually slow—at first pain may only be mild after training. Untreated, the pain often progresses to a stage when all weight bearing activity is painful. Persistent training with shin pain may lead to stress fractures. It is wise to seek intervention at the earliest possible stage. Although there are many different causes of shin splints, the condition generally falls into the category of overuse injuries. Like all overuse injuries, shin splints is the inflammatory response of a structure unable to withstand the repetitive loads that are placed on it. The aggravating factor can usually be tracked down to a change in one of the four aspects of training: technique, intensity/duration, training surface, or equipment and the condition is managed by modifying the variable that has brought about the pain. This may mean anything from training on a softer surface, to changing the footwear, to altering the athlete's way of performing an activity. Often shin splints will occur due to predisposing physical factors such as poor foot control, tight musculature in the lower limb, or weakness in muscle controlling movement of the lower limb. These should be assessed and treated by a physiotherapist or sports physician. The symptoms of shin splints can be treated with the PRICED regime and stretching.

Prevention The likelihood of being affected by shin splints can be reduced by regular stretching of the calf and shin muscles before and after training. Regular massage or self-massage of the calf muscles also helps maintain flexibility. Intensity and duration of exercise should be progressed gradually throughout the training program to give the body time to adapt to the extra loading. A soft or yielding training surface and good footwear will lessen the impact forces which have to be absorbed by the body. Poor running technique can also be a predisposing factor; video analysis may help in highlighting problems before they get to injury stage.

Swimmer's shoulder

Management Commonly this ailment involves irritation and inflammation of one of the tendons which pass under the shoulder. The pain is most often felt at the front of the shoulder but may be felt behind. Pain which co-exists in the neck, upper back or down the arm should be immediately diagnosed. In some cases X-rays and anti-inflammatory medication may be necessary. The mechanism of the injury, which falls into the category of overuse, usually occurs in the presence of predisposing structure (anatomy) and the swimmer's individual stroke completion (biomechanics). For most such injuries, modification of training with a lessening of intensity and volume is required in conjunction with PRICED to reduce symptoms. Early intervention will mean less training will be missed. A quality program of stretching should be implemented for both the warm-up and warm-down as well as for therapy. Every session should conclude with a regime of icing.

Prevention A full assessment of the length and strength of the musculature of the shoulder is often necessary. The length and strength tests of the muscles fall into three groups; arm to chest, arm to shoulder blade, and back to shoulder blade. Abnormalities in the range of upper back and neck joints and nerve tissue may greatly affect muscle action and therefore also require examination. Individual assessment and specific programs of stretching are important. Imbalances in the length and strength of these muscle groups result in poorly co-ordinated muscle contractions which often lead to excessive movement of the ball of the shoulder (usually up and forward). In the presence of repeated poor stroking, this may lead to a trapping of the tendons under the point of the shoulder causing pain and inflammation. Video analysis of an athlete's technique by the coach may identify other faults such as excessive body roll or a lack of elbow height in arm recovery. Poor technique is often the result of muscular and joint stiffness which, left uncorrected, will lead to worsening or recurrence of the symptoms. Attempts at stroke correction will be unsuccessful unless the individual's muscle and joint problems are attended to.

Retro-patellar pain (runner's knee)

Management Athletes will often complain of pain in the vicinity of the kneecap. The onset of pain is usually gradual and associated with a change in intensity, frequency or duration of training. Runner's knee may be the result of the body adjusting to altered training or to a change of footwear. This injury can be considered in the overuse category, often predisposed by anatomical problems (anatomy) or faulty technique (biomechanics). It is unlikely that modification of training alone will alleviate symptoms on a permanent basis. With all musculoskeletal pain, accurate diagnosis is always the key to effective management. Intervention early in the inflammation and pain cycle with appropriate stretching, PRICED, and, if necessary, anti-inflammatory medication, will usually settle the problem. A specific regime of patello-femoral taping to correct kneecap movement has proven very beneficial. If management is instituted early and effec-tively, minimal training will be lost. Any quality stretching program will aim to correct those inflexibilities which are predisposing the athlete toward injury. This program may also include exercises to encourage better use of previously under-used muscles, thus improving technique.

Prevention A full assessment of the length and strength of the musculature of the pelvis, hip and leg is often necessary. The muscles of particular importance are the hip flexors, the gluteals, the quadriceps, the hamstrings and the calves. A quality therapeutic program of stretching, self massage and muscular control exercises should result from this assessment. Drills to improve running and jumping technique should be commenced and integrated into the athlete's training pro-gram. The presence of abnormal foot structure which changes the amount of rotation in the thigh and leg could predispose the athlete to injury. Video assessment may be reviewed by the coach, sports physiotherapist and sports podiatrist, and orthotic treatment may be required. These changes will alleviate the problem and they may also improve overall performance.

Sporting injuries can largely be avoided if correct care is taken during practice and games. Correctly preparing the body for the activity it is about to perform and heeding the safety standards of the sport will help reduce the risk of injury, although it is inevitable that some injuries will occur. When this happens, it is important to be competent in the assessment and immediate first aid management of that injury. The initial treatment of an injury may be the most critical factor in determining its severity and thus the length of time the athlete must spend away from sport. The basic guidelines presented in this chapter can be safely followed for efficient management of minor injuries. In the event of a more serious injury get qualified medical assessment. Courses are run by sports medicine organisations for those wishing to further their knowledge in injury prevention and management.

SUMMARY

- The most important principle of injury treatment is prevention.
- Injuries can be largely prevented through skill development, obeying the rules of the sport, well-maintained playing facilities, use of protective devices, allowing for varying environmental conditions, not exercising when sick, ensuring appropriate levels of specific fitness, and using correct warm-up and warm-down techniques.
- Warming-up should consist of a general warm-up (e.g. jogging), followed by static and ballistic stretching. More specific warm-ups that mimic the actual skills, movements and intensities of the event or sport should then be performed.
- Warm-downs should consist of both a general warm-down of light aerobic activity for 5–10 minutes, followed by static stretching of the muscle groups used in the sport or activity.
- Treatment of an athletic injury follows three phases: inflammation (up to 72 hours), repair (up to six weeks) and remodelling. A number of things should be avoided following an injury, especially during the inflammatory stage; these include heat, alcohol, exercise and massage.

- The initial treatment of an injury is the most critical factor in determining an injury's severity and thus the length of time an athlete will be unable to compete.

RECOMMENDED READING

Alter, M.J. (1990) *Sport Stretch*, Leisure Press, Champaign, Illinois.

Arnheim, D. and W.E. Prentice (1993) *Principles of Athletic Training* Mosby Yearbook, St Louis.

Bloomfield, J., P.A. Fricker and K.D. Fitch (eds) (1995) *Science and Medicine in Sport* Blackwell Scientific Publications, Melbourne.

Bruckner, P. and K. Khan (1993) *Clinical Sports Medicine* McGraw-Hill, Sydney.

8

Nutrition for speed and endurance

Greg Cox, Holly Frail and Kerry Leech

Proper nutrition should be an integral part of every athlete's training and competition program. An incorrect balance of energy sources, nutrients and fluids will significantly impair endurance, strength, power, speed, body composition, recovery, concentration and general health. If nutrition is not included as an integral part of training and preparation for competition, then even the most talented individuals may never reach their full sporting potential. This chapter will provide detailed information on dietary intake for the athlete, with advice on the intake of carbohydrate, protein, fat and minerals. Other special issues addressed include considerations for the female athlete, tips on bulking-up, advice to the vegetarian athlete and the inclusion of alcohol. Food and fluid intake before, during and following exercise are outlined; finally, there is a section on the most popular ergogenic aids currently used by athletes to improve their performance.

To achieve optimal nutritional status for peak sporting performance, athletes must ensure they consume an adequate carbohydrate intake, avoid an excessive fat intake, consume adequate (not excessive) amounts of protein-rich foods, maintain optimal fluid balance, consume adequate vitamins and minerals, maintain or reach a desired weight or body fat level, plan ahead for pre-match meals and nutrition recovery techniques, and avoid excessive alcohol consumption.

Despite the attention sport nutrition currently receives, many athletes have dietary habits which are less than ideal for optimal training and competition performance. Every athlete needs to make informed nutrition choices to ensure maximum improvements with training, ultimately peaking in competition.

PRINCIPLES OF THE TRAINING DIET

Although 95% of an athlete's waking hours can be spent training, most athletes focus on diet only during the competition phase and fail to meet their nutritional needs while training. Remember, training provides the platform from which athletes are able to compete at their best.

The training diet must meet fuel and nutrient needs during high energy expenditure, establish long-term eating habits for nutritional benefit, maintain an appropriate fat to lean mass ratio, promote optimal recovery and practice strategies for eating during competitions.

Energy

The major change in nutritional requirements for the athlete in training is the need for extra fuel (i.e. kilojoules). The extent to which energy requirements increase varies greatly between individuals, being dependent on age, sex, size, growth status, basal metabolic rate (BMR) and activity. For example, metabolic rate is higher in men compared with women; it is also higher during periods of growth and development and tends to decrease with age.

Energy intake should be balanced with energy expenditure. This enables the athlete to reach and maintain the ideal body weight and body fat level. Energy intake should also keep pace with the extra demands of training, growth and development of muscle tissue. BMR is the energy used at

Table 8.1: Activities as described by multiples of BMR		
Activity category	**Energy cost**	**Range**
Moderate activities	4.0	3.0–5.0
cycling (slowly), cricket, horse riding		
Strenuous	7.0	5.0–9.0
tennis (fast pace), swimming (moderate),		
aerobics, football, running, weight training		
Very strenuous	10.0	7.0–13.0
swimming (race pace), rowing, cycling,		
squash (fast pace), running		

rest; as we increase our activity, energy use must also increase. Table 8.1 lists various activities as multiples of BMR.

Athletes require up to 200–300 kilojoules per kilogram of body weight per day. For some this may represent a daily intake of as much as 21 000 kilojoules (5 000 calories). A major problem for these athletes, particularly those who have yet to finish growing, is to consume adequate amounts of food while timing meals to fit in with training, work or study. Difficulties may arise here due to lack of knowledge, appetite, time and/or food preparation skills. Ideally, 5 or 6 smaller meals/snacks should be eaten over the day (i.e. eating every 2 to 3 hours). Liquid foods such as sports drinks (e.g. Isosport, Gatorade) or liquid meal supplements (e.g. Sustagen) are useful in providing the extra energy demands required for training.

Athletes involved in sports with low energy expenditure (e.g. jockeys) may find it difficult to balance energy intake with energy expenditure while meeting other nutritional requirements. In these circumstances, the athlete will have to concentrate on ensuring that all the food eaten provides quality nutrition, with nutritious carbohydrate and protein-rich foods forming the basis of the training diet.

Athletes who do not meet their energy requirements are likely to suffer from weight loss (particularly decreased lean muscle tissue), fatigue, increased risk of overtraining and a decreased ability to recover between training sessions. They will also be at greater risk of not achieving vitamin, mineral and protein requirements. It is vital to maintain a balanced diet irrespective of the nutritional goals. The ideal composition of daily energy intake for athletes is at least 55–60% of

Table 8.2: Estimated daily carbohydrate requirements

General sport and activities up to 60 minutes training per day of low intensity	5–6g/kg (i.e. 5–6 grams of carbohydrate for every kilogram of body weight)
Moderate 60–120 minutes of high intensity or lengthy medium intensity	6–8 g/kg body weight
Endurance greater than 120 minutes high intensity	9–10 g/kg body weight
Extreme 5–6 hours of intense exercise	12–13 g/kg body weight

kilojoules from carbohydrate, less than 30% from fat and 12–15% from protein.

Carbohydrates

Carbohydrates (in the form of glucose and glycogen) are the most readily available fuel source used by the working muscles of both speed and endurance athletes. They are the preferred fuel for most types of training. When exercising anaerobically (i.e. during high intensity activities), carbohydrates are used almost exclusively by the working muscles to provide energy for work. In endurance-based activities, carbohydrates are a vital fuel source for the aerobic pathways which produce the energy necessary for sustained muscular work.

Lack of carbohydrate in the diet leads to inadequate glycogen stores (stored carbohydrate) in the muscles and liver, contributing to an inability to maintain blood glucose levels and provide adequate fuel for the working muscles. This leads to early fatigue, loss of concentration, poor recovery, and possibly headaches and nausea. Full muscle and liver, glycogen stores are essential for maintaining high work intensity during both training and competition. Athletes who train daily (or twice daily) require at least 5–10 grams of carbohydrate per kilogram of body weight per day. The exact amount of carbohydrate required will vary from athlete to athlete according to their level of training and competition. General estimations of daily carbohydrate requirements for various athletes are listed in Table 8.2.

To meet carbohydrate needs, frequent small meals centred around nutritious carbohydrate foods should be eaten

---

Table 8.3: Daily carbohydrate calculation

Assume a 70 kg endurance athlete training twice daily. Training includes running, cycling, swimming and weights. Sessions are 90–120 minutes in duration.

Estimated daily carbohydrate requirements are 9 grams of carbohydrate per kilogram of body weight (from Table 8.2).

To calculate carbohydrate requirements, multiply body weight (70kg) by grams of carbohydrate required per kilogram of body weight (9g/kg body weight).

Carbohydrate requirements = 70 × 9 = 630 grams of carbohydrate per day

---

throughout the day. Small amounts of simple sugars (no more than 5–10% of total energy intake) may be helpful during periods of high energy expenditure (e.g. during a heavy training phase); these may include sweet spreads such as jam and honey, and sweetened drinks such as cordials, soft drinks, fruit juices and sport drinks. Excess refined carbohydrates and sugars however, can lead to vitamin, mineral and fibre deficiencies. However, high sugar items that are also high in fat (e.g. chocolate, pastries and rich desserts), should only be used as occasional extras.

Those athletes with very high carbohydrate requirements may need to use high carbohydrate fluids and supplements to reach an adequate energy intake. These supplements may include sports drinks (e.g. Isosport, Gatorade), commercial liquid meal supplements (e.g. Sustagen Sport) and the wide variety of sports bars (e.g. Power Bar). Refer to Table 8.3 for an example of daily carbohydrate requirement calculation.

Strength, speed and endurance athletes must consume adequate quantities of carbohydrate on a daily basis, because repeated bouts of anaerobic (high intensity) exercise and prolonged aerobic (endurance) exercise place high demands on muscle carbohydrate (glycogen) stores. Table 8.4 presents a list of foods that each provide 50 grams of carbohydrate.

Carbohydrate intake during longer training sessions (e.g. 90 minutes or more), involving repeated bouts of high intensity exercise (e.g. weight training, interval training) or continuous moderate intensity exercise (e.g. cycling, jogging), helps prevent muscle and liver glycogen depletion and delays fatigue. This form of supplementation during exercise can be in the form of carbohydrate-containing fluids such as sport drinks, dilute cordials and fruit juices. It is also

Table 8.4: 50g serves of carbohydrate

Food	Quantity	Food	Quantity
Bread and cereals			
Bread	4 slices	Crumpet	2 average
Pocket bread	2 average	Pasta (cooked)	1.5 cups
Cooked rice	1.5 cups	Untoasted muesli	1 cup
Weet-Bix/Vitabrits	4 biscuits	All Bran	1 cup
Flakes with fruit	1.5 cups	Sustain	1 cup
Oats (cooked)	2.25 cups	Oats (raw)	0.75 cup
Fruit muffin	1.5 average	Breakfast bar	2 bars
Crispbread	8 large	Scone	2–3 average
Pikelets	4 average	Pancake	2 large
Muesli bar	2.5 bars		
Dairy products			
Fruit yoghurt	2 tubs (400g)	Yoghurt (plain)	3 tubs (600g)
Milk (all types)	1 litre	Skim milk powder	5 tbsp
Starchy vegetables			
Corn	2 cups	Potato (cooked)	2 large
Lentils/kidney beans	1.5 cups	Baked beans	1.5 cups
Fruit			
Bananas	2 large	Apricots	10 medium
Apples/oranges/pears	3 average	Grapes	2 medium bunches
Peaches	6 medium	Strawberries	3.5 cups
Melon	3.5 cups	Mango	1 large
Dates	9	Apricots	10 whole or 20 halves
Sultanas	6 tbsp	Fruit salad	2 cups
Tinned fruit	2 cups	Fruit snack pack	3
Miscellaneous products			
Honey/golden syrup/jam	2 tbsp	Sports bar (e.g. Power Bar)	1 average
Fruit Roll-up	4	Sugar	2 tbsp
Beverages and liquid supplements			
Softdrink/cordial	500 ml	Fruit juice	600 ml
Glucose powder/Glucodin	2.5 tbsp	Sustagen	4 tbsp
Polycose/Maximum	2.5 tbsp	Sustagen with milk	2 tbsp + 300 ml milk
Ensure Plus	1 can	Sustagen tetrapak	1.5 packs
Sports drinks (e.g. Isosport, Gatorade, Exceed)	750–800 ml	Meal replacement fluid (e.g. Exceed sports nutrition supplement, GatorPro)	1 can/tetrapak
Ensure Powder (lactose free)	80g		

Table 8.5: High and low glycaemic index foods

High	Low
Rice Bubbles, Cornflakes	Porridge, Sultana Bran
Puffed Wheat, Weet-Bix	Long grain white rice
Wholemeal and white bread	Instant noodles, pasta
Puffed crispbread, water crackers	Fruit loaf, mixed grain bread
Calrose and Sunbrown quick rice	Lentils, kidney beans, baked beans
Glucose, honey	Apple, apricot, grapes, peach, orange
Lucozade, jelly beans	Milk, yoghurt
Banana, watermelon	Fructose (fruit sugar)

Source: Adapted from 'Glycaemic Index—an update and overview', in Nutrition Issues and Abstracts, No. 6, June 1995.

recommended that athletes consume a carbohydrate-based drink and/or snack within 10–30 minutes of completing any training or competition session. Research indicates that an intake of approximately 1 gram of carbohydrate per kilogram body weight during this time will enable the body to rapidly replace muscle glycogen stores. This is essential for maintaining heavy workloads during busy training and competition schedules.

Carbohydrates can be either simple or complex. It has been generally assumed up to now that simple carbohydrates are released quickly into the bloodstream, causing a rapid rise in blood sugar levels, while complex carbohydrates are released more slowly, resulting in a more even blood sugar level. Recent scientific evidence has shown that this explanation is misleading and that the availability of carbohydrate from a food is better explained by its glycaemic index (GI). The GI of a food refers to its rate of glucose (carbohydrate) uptake from the digestive system. Carbohydrates from food with a high GI are released quickly into the bloodstream, while carbohydrates from food with a low GI are released more slowly. Athletes are now advised to choose foods with a low GI before exercise (for the slow release of sugar into the bloodstream) and foods with higher GI during the recovery period (for fast repletion of muscle and liver glycogen stores). Further research is required in this area to determine the full extent to which GI can be applied to the athlete. Table 8.5 provides a list of foods with high and low GI.

Table 8.6: Daily protein requirements	
Sedentary	0.8g/kg body weight
Strength athlete	1.5–2.0 g/kg body weight
Endurance athlete	1.5–1.6g/kg body weight
Note: Adequate energy intake is also essential.	

Protein

To cope with the added demands of exercise, athletes use slightly more protein than non-athletes. In most cases this additional protein is provided by the increased total energy intake required for exercise, provided the diet is balanced. Protein is required for growth, maintenance and repair of all the body's tissues. The recommended dietary intake for protein appears in Table 8.6.

Strength and speed athletes who need to increase lean body mass (muscle) must consume a diet high in carbo-hydrate, moderate in protein and low in fat in combination with specific resistance training. In most exercise tasks, protein is a minor source of energy, however, in a glyco-gen-depleted state, e.g. during the latter stages of exhaustive exercise, protein can play a larger role in providing energy for the working muscles. This contribution to total energy expenditure can be as great as 5–10%.

It is important to realise that a balanced diet will provide sufficient protein to cover these additional requirements. If the diet is not balanced, however, insufficient protein intake could contribute to fatigue through an inability to build and maintain muscle mass, as well as leading to slow recovery following injury.

The most effective way to meet daily protein demands is to spread protein intake over five small meals per day with no more than approximately 35 grams of protein in any one meal or snack. If large amounts of protein are consumed at one meal, the excess will be converted to, and stored as, fat. Excess protein may also increase urinary calcium excretion which may be dangerous to females and young athletes.

Meeting the goals of protein intake should be accompa-nied by meeting other general nutrition goals, especially where total energy intake needs to be low. Many food sources of protein also provide valuable nutrients such as calcium, iron and zinc. Animal sources of protein include meat, poultry, fish and seafood, eggs and dairy products; these provide the best quality and balance of amino acids. Plant sources of protein include breads, breakfast cereals, rice, pasta, legumes and pulses, and commercially prepared vegetarian meat alternatives (e.g. Nutmeat, Rediburger); however, these plant sources often provide incomplete ranges of the essential amino acids and are best combined with animal sources. That said, a vegetarian diet can be entirely adequate in protein as long as it is well planned, balanced and includes a variety of protein sources. Special nutrition issues for the vegetarian athlete are discussed later in this chapter.

Fat

Small amounts of dietary fat provide essential fatty acids for energy and fat-soluble vitamins to maintain body functions. Fat is predominantly used as an energy source during long low-intensity exercise and supplies twice the kilojoules as the same amount of carbohydrate and protein. However, all athletes have more than adequate fat stores for exercise, irrespective of their leanness. Excess dietary fat intake may lead to the storage of excess body fat (and increased body weight) and a lowering of muscle glycogen levels, which may lead to early fatigue during exercise.

There has recently been some debate concerning the use of high fat diets during training and competition to improve endurance performance through increased fat oxidation during exercise. The research in this area, however, has focused on non-elite athletes exercising at low intensities of exercise (60% of VO_2 max). At present there is insufficient evidence to support the idea of 'fat loading' for the athlete competing in endurance events at intensities of 70–80% VO_2 max (which is typical of race pace). It is more likely that endurance athletes may impair rather than enhance their performance by eating fat at the expense of carbohydrates. More controlled studies are required over longer periods of time to clarify this issue.

Vitamins and minerals

Both vitamins and minerals are required in small amounts for optimal performance and health. Vitamin and mineral deficiencies lead to early fatigue, increased susceptibility to illness and infections, and slow recovery from wounds and injury. Vitamins do not themselves supply energy (kilojoules). They do, however, help produce energy from fuels such as fat and carbohydrate, help produce red blood cells, and promote tissue repair. No well-controlled scientific trial has yet been able to show that increased vitamin intake, over and above that provided by a normal well-balanced diet, will enhance sporting performance. There is always the possibility of a 'placebo' (psychological) effect with supplementation.

Vitamin deficiencies which occur with athletes are usually a result of poor dietary choices or inadequate energy intake. Adequate intake of vitamins and minerals is best ensured and most economically achieved by improving the diet rather than by buying and consuming supplements. Table 8.7 lists major food sources of various vitamins and minerals.

Athletes rely heavily on vitamins C and the B-complex (water-soluble vitamins). Vitamin C plays an important role in stress control and resistance to infection, while a major function of the B-group vitamins is in energy metabolism for muscular work. The chief sources of these nutrients are fresh fruit and vegetables, wholegrain breads and cereals, lean meats and dairy products. As athletes increase their carbohydrate intake and consume adequate protein, they will naturally obtain more of these nutrients in their normal daily intake.

While a moderate excess of vitamins B and C will simply be excreted in the urine, prolonged use of megadoses (more than 50–100 times the recommended daily intake) may lead to a dependency on larger amounts of the vitamin, or could impair the action or absorption of another related vitamin. In contrast to water-soluble vitamins, fat-soluble vitamins (particularly vitamins A, D, and K), are stored in the body and can become toxic if supplemented in large doses.

Recent research has focused on the role played by supplements of antioxidants (such as Vitamins A, C and E)

Table 8.7: Major vitamin and mineral sources

Vitamin A: yellow and orange fruit and vegetables, eggs, dairy products, margarine and oils

B Vitamins: wholegrain bread and cereals, brown rice and pastas, Vegemite, lean meats, dairy products, green leafy vegetables

Vitamin C: citrus, tropical and berry fruits, red capsicum and tomatoes

Vitamin E: wholegrain bread & cereals, wheatgerm, nuts & seeds, unsaturated oils

Iron: organ meats (e.g. liver), beef and other meats, turkey, chicken, fish and seafood. To a lesser extent: eggs, green leafy vegetables, iron enriched breads and cereals, dried fruit, legumes
For iron intake: eat lean red meat 2–3 times per week and include a source of vitamin C at that meal

Calcium: dairy products and fortified soy milks (e.g. So Good, Good Life)
Lesser sources: fish, dark green vegetables, nuts and seeds, wholegrains
For calcium intake: adults—500ml milk + 200g yoghurt (or 1 slice cheese); children and adolescents—750ml milk and 200g yoghurt (or 1 slice cheese)

---

in preventing cell damage (muscle soreness) after intense exercise at altitude and in heavily polluted environments. As their role is as yet unproven, the best choices are foods high in these nutrients. Good sources include green leafy vegetables, vegetable oils/margarines, citrus and tropical fruits, wheatgerm and nuts.

Athletes consuming a high-energy well-balanced diet should easily be able to obtain the vitamins and minerals they require without resorting to supplementation. However, those athletes who undertake intense training programs, are on weight reduction diets, are strict vegetarians, have restricted diets, are pregnant or breastfeeding, may benefit from sensible supplementation. This should be from a well-balanced multi-vitamin/mineral supplement or from more specific supplementation on advice from a sports medicine doctor or sports dietitian. For example, it may be sensible to take a supplement when travelling to compete, particularly overseas, where the nutritional content of the local food may be unknown.

Iron

Due to its important role in oxygen transport in the blood and muscles, iron is essential in the athlete's diet. Those athletes who reduce their intake of one of the best iron sources (lean red meat) because they consider it to be high in fat and cholesterol may leave themselves at risk of low iron stores and perhaps iron-deficiency anaemia. Symptoms of the latter include excessive fatigue, breathlessness, cramps and decreased resistance to infection.

Iron deficiency and impaired athletic performance is most common in women (due to their increased iron loss through menstruation) and vegetarians. Others who may be at risk of iron depletion include those who suffer frequent nose bleeds or who have had an illness or medication associated with blood loss. High impact exercise may also be associated with higher iron turnover and lower iron intakes (poor diet, low energy intake). Although many athletes may be iron-depleted to some degree, and true deficiency is rare, all athletes with low iron status should be treated as having potential iron depletion or deficiency. 'At risk' athletes should have regular blood tests through a sports physician to check their haemoglobin and ferritin (iron storage) levels to see whether they require supplementation.

All athletes should be encouraged to consume iron-rich foods. Dietary iron comes in two forms: haem iron, such as organ (liver, kidney) and red meats, poultry, fish and seafood; and non-haem, such as legumes (kidney beans, lentils), eggs, wholegrain and fortified cereals (Weet-Bix, Vitabrits, Sustain, Special K) and dark green vegetables (spinach, broccoli). Haem iron sources are more readily absorbed by the body than other sources. Consuming a source of vitamin C (e.g. citrus fruit or juice, berry fruits) at the same meal as meat enhances iron absorption. It is worth knowing, too, that the tannins in tea and phytates in high fibre foods (e.g. excess added brans) are factors which inhibit the absorption of iron.

Calcium

Calcium is essential for the growth and strength of the skeletal system, as well as for muscle contraction. The best sources are dairy products, since the lactose in dairy products aids in calcium absorption. To avoid excess fat and kilojoules, choose reduced fat dairy products. Some individuals, especially those with milk allergies, may need to use fortified soy milk alternatives (e.g. So Good, Good Life) or take calcium supplements.

Extra attention has been focused on dietary calcium intake for female athletes due to concern about the relationship between sports amenorrhoea, osteopenia (decreased bone mass), stress fractures and calcium intake. Although a precise understanding of all the causes and consequences of these conditions is yet to be reached, much of the current evidence supports a higher calcium intake for female athletes to decrease the risk of decreased bone density. For some, this may mean the use of supplements.

SPECIAL ISSUES

The female athlete

With increased numbers of female athletes competing at both the elite and social levels, greater interest has now centred on issues, often nutrition-based, relating to the female athlete. A major concern for women is matching the energy requirements of an individual sport with the nutritional requirements of the athlete. A complicating factor is the social pressure often placed on female athletes to achieve a certain 'look' or 'body type' which is construed as being desirable for performance and appearance.

Sports in which weight control is important (e.g. lightweight rowing, judo) and for which low energy intakes are required, involve greater responsibility on the female athlete to ensure that quality food choices are made and that protein, iron and calcium requirements are met. For some athletes with low energy intakes, vitamin and mineral supplementation may be needed.

Losing body fat

Carrying extra body fat will disadvantage most athletes. An over-fat athlete will have a decreased power-to-weight ratio, decreased endurance, strength, speed and agility, all factors which significantly influence sporting performance. Increased levels of body fat may even become psychologically negative in some individuals. It should be noted that normal height–weight charts and weighing scales are not the best measures of determining ideal weight or measuring the progress of the athlete. Anthropometry and, in particular, skinfold measurements, sometimes combined with circumferences or the 'O-scale' method, are more appropriate for gauging changes in body composition in response to training.

The main causes of being overweight are:

- Consuming excess total kilojoules, particularly in the later part of the day.
- Consuming excess fat or alcohol.
- Skipping meals, especially breakfast and lunch.
- Bingeing between meals or late at night.

The most effective way for the athlete to lose weight or body fat is to:

- Aim for no more than 0.5–1 kg loss in body weight per week; a loss of lean muscle tissue may occur if weight loss is more rapid than this.
- Spread food intake over 5–6 small meals per day rather than 2–3 larger meals.
- Follow a balanced diet, ensuring adequate energy for training and adequate carbohydrate (particularly high fibre choices) to maintain glycogen stores and satisfy the appetite.
- Decrease consumption of fats, alcohol and excess refined sugars, which provide the highest kilojoule content for the lowest nutrient value.
- Spread protein intake over the entire day.
- Change poor eating habits such as eating when bored, stressed, depressed, celebrating, or merely due to habit, social occasions or other environmental or social reasons.

- Allow planned 'treats' to avoid any episodes of bingeing.
- Include longer lower-intensity exercise as an integral component of a general conditioning phase of a training program (e.g. pre-season training).
- Monitor body fat levels on a regular basis (e.g. every 2–3 months is ideal).

Bulking up

Many athletes, particularly males involved in strength-related sports, strive to gain kilograms and increase their muscle mass. Hypertrophy (increased mass) of skeletal muscle generally increases strength and power, provides an improved ability to withstand some injuries, and may even provide a psychological advantage over the opposition through perceived superior physical presence.

The main reasons that some individuals find it difficult to gain a desired increase in muscle mass can be attributed to:

- Insufficient energy (kilojoule) intake.
- Inadequate number of meals and snacks during the course of the day.
- Excessive training or energy used in other activities such as physical work or other sports.
- Physical immaturity and adolescent growth spurts.
- Inappropriate training practices.
- Genetic potential.

Tips for bulking up include:

- Following a well-planned resistance training program.
- Having at least 5 or 6 meals per day and consuming more kilojoules than those expended. Liquid meals may be useful in some situations.
- Consuming small to moderate serves of protein at each meal to facilitate muscle maintenance and growth.
- Consuming a source of carbohydrate and protein immediately following a resistance-training session to facilitate recovery. This practice will promote optimal muscle glyco-

gen replenishment and maximise muscle growth and development.

Athletes should ensure that their bulking-up diet is relatively low in fat, otherwise the weight may be gained as extra body fat (especially in older age groups). High carbohydrate, but perhaps lower fibre, foods and drinks should be consumed with and between meals. Sugars should be used sensibly to add extra kilojoules. In addition, extra kilojoules and protein can be added to drinks by mixing in a couple of tablespoons of skim milk powder (which is very cheap), or some other protein powder or high energy drink mix (e.g. Sustagen, Exceed Sports Meal). Blend in fruit, yoghurt, icecream, honey, etc. for extra flavour. If possible, extra snacks such as banana sandwiches, dried fruit and nut mixes or extra milk drinks should be consumed between meals and training sessions. Although monitoring body fat levels is a difficult task, athletes should be encouraged to do this to ensure that their gains in body weight are due to increases in lean muscle tissue rather than fat. Above all, they must be patient; gains of 1–2 kilograms per month are excellent.

EATING DISORDERS

The prevalence of eating disorders has increased both in the general community and amongst the athletic population. Eating disorders include both the clinical syndromes of anorexia nervosa and bulimia nervosa but at times doctors and coaches may find it difficult to distinguish between an eating disorder and an athlete following the guidelines for eating and exercise. Many athletes, especially female athletes, are compulsive in both their eating and training habits and may be terrified of gaining body fat. These athletes should be identified and provided with dietary assistance from a sports dietitian, in conjunction with a sports physician, to overcome their fears.

THE VEGETARIAN ATHLETE

Athletes who are vegetarian choose to avoid meat and other animal-derived products for a variety of reasons. Vegetarians are classified depending on the types of food they exclude from their diets and include:

- Vegans, who consume foods derived only from the plant kingdom.
- Lacto-vegetarians, who consume dairy produce plus plant derived foods.
- Lacto-ovo-vegetarians, who consume dairy produce and eggs plus plant derived foods.
- Ovo-vegetarians, who consume eggs plus plant derived foods.

Vegetarian athletes, and even athletes who follow a mixed diet, may fail to meet all their nutrient requirements if they do not plan their daily food choices adequately. At risk for vegetarian athletes include energy and protein requirements, vitamin B_{12}, iron, calcium and zinc. It is most important that vegetarian athletes make informed food choices. The vegetarian athletes at most risk of inadequate dietary intakes are those who simply exclude meat from their diet and make little or no effort to find suitable vegetarian alternatives. These individuals have been described as 'pseudo vegetarians' who often have excluded meat for fear of excess dietary fat.

Energy

A common problem for the vegetarian athlete is how to consume adequate energy (kilojoules) throughout the day to cope with the added demands of training. This is most common in the vegan athlete as many of the foods available to them are high bulk and low energy dense (e.g. legumes, breads and cereals, fruit and vegetables). This problem can be easily overcome if a variety of energy dense foods are included on a daily basis, such as nuts, commercially prepared vegetarian meat alternatives (e.g. Sanitarium Nutmeat,

Table 8.8: Approximately 10 grams of protein is provided by the following foods

Food	Quantity
Nuts (mixed)	50g
Nutmeat	50g
Tempeh	50g
Textured vegetable protein (TVP)	70g (1/2 cup)
Lentils (boiled)	150g (3/4 cup)
Kidney beans	150g (3/4 cup)
Skim milk	300ml
Soy milk (fortified)	300ml
Non-fat fruit yoghurt	200g carton
Bread	4 slices
Pasta/noodles	2 cups

Rediburger), and fortified soy milks (e.g. So Good, Good Life).

Protein

A common misconception amongst vegetarians is that protein foods should be complemented at each meal to ensure an adequate supply of the amino acids essential for muscle growth, development and repair. All they need to do is include a variety of protein foods throughout the day. There is no need to complement protein foods at any one particular meal. Table 8.8 provides a list of vegetarian protein-rich foods that provide 10 grams of protein.

Vitamin B_{12}

As requirements for vitamin B_{12} are extremely small, and much of the body's requirement is secreted and reabsorbed in the small intestine, only vegans are recommended to take vitamin B_{12} supplements. Products fortified with B_{12} include So Good Soy Drink, Good Life Non-Dairy Soy Drink.

Iron

As iron absorption is relatively low from non haem sources (mainly plant sources), vegetarian athletes of all types need to be conscious of non haem iron sources and how to maximise iron intake from these foods. The major sources of iron for vegetarian athletes are meat alternatives such as textured vegetable protein (TVP), Sanitarium Rediburger and Longlife Vege-Hotdogs, legumes, eggs, green leafy vegetables, nuts and seeds and wholegrain cereals, especially those which have been fortified with iron (e.g. Sustain, Special K).

Calcium

Major calcium sources for the vegetarian athlete are dairy products. The vegan athlete, however, must rely on calcium fortified soy milks (So Good Soy Drink, Good Life Non-Dairy Soy Drink), tofu, nuts and seeds, fortified breakfast cereals and dark green vegetables low in oxalic acid (as oxalic acid tends to inhibit calcium absorption).

Zinc

Good sources of zinc for the vegetarian athlete include legumes, nuts and seeds, wholegrain breads and cereals, wheatgerm, and vegetarian meat alternatives.

ALCOHOL

Alcohol is an integral part of many sports at both the elite and social level. Many athletes enjoy a drink with other competitors and team members, usually following a game or competition. If other nutritional goals are kept in mind while enjoying 'a drink', alcohol can be part of an athlete's winning diet.

Consumption of alcohol immediately after competition:

- Leads to further dehydration, not fluid replacement.
- Suppresses glycogen replacement.
- Provides minimal carbohydrate (e.g. 50g carbohydrate = 4 stubbies beer).
- Exacerbates soft tissue injuries by increasing swelling and bruising, therefore slowing recovery.

- Increases the loss of important vitamins and minerals (e.g. zinc) essential for injury recovery and immunity to infection.

To aid recovery and repair following a game or competition, alcohol should be avoided *until* fluid and carbohydrate needs are replaced, and then consumed in moderation. Alcohol should be avoided *completely* if the athlete has suffered an injury, illness or significant fatigue during the competition.

PREPARATION FOR COMPETITION

Preparation for competition involves refining the diet to maximise fuel (glycogen) and fluid stores. For endurance athletes to achieve this, they must increase carbohydrate intake while decreasing protein and fat consumption over the 2 or 3 days before the event while the intensity and duration of training is reduced.

True carbohydrate loading is of most benefit to athletes competing in events lasting more than 90 minutes. It may also be useful for some team players in preparation for a day, weekend or week of competition where many games or events are involved. Carbohydrate loading may be carried out for 3 or more days before the competition, depending on the length of and time of the taper, by taking in 10 grams of carbohydrate for every kilogram of their body weight each day. This allows the muscles to store 2 or 3 times the normal amount of glycogen. Refer to Table 8.9 for a sample daily food intake for a 70kg athlete carbohydrate loading.

Team players involved in a weekly competition should maintain a high carbohydrate intake throughout the training week leading up to a weekend game or match. For these athletes there is little benefit in carbohydrate loading 1 or 2 days before a weekend match. Adequate carbohydrate should be eaten throughout the entire week to cope with daily training demands in preparation for the weekend competition.

Table 8.9: A sample intake for a 70kg athlete carbohydrate loading prior to an event. The target is to consume 10g of carbohydrate per kilogram of body weight per day (i.e. 700 grams of carbohydrate per day).

Breakfast	1 glass of fruit juice
	6 Weet-Bix/Vitabrits or 2 cups of breakfast cereal
	1 cup of reduced fat or low fat milk
	2 slices of toast (unbuttered) with jam/honey
	1 medium banana
Morning snack	2 crumpets (unbuttered) with jam/honey
	750 ml of sports drink (e.g. Isosport, Gatorade)
Lunch	2 large bread rolls or 6 slices of bread (unbuttered) with salad
	1 piece of fruit
	1 glass of cordial
Afternoon snack	200 grams of low fat fruit yoghurt
	1 fruit muffin or sandwich (unbuttered) with jam/honey/Vegemite
Evening meal	2 cups of cooked rice (with lean beef and vegetable stir-fry)
	2 slices of bread
	1 cup of fruit salad and 200g tub of low fat fruit yoghurt
Supper	2 slices of raisin toast with jam or honey (unbuttered)
	1 glass of reduced fat or low fat milk.

Total energy intake 15700 kJ, providing 705g carbohydrate (i.e. 75% of energy intake as carbohydrate).

By the day of competition, and with glycogen stores filled to capacity, the pre-event meal should be composed of easily digestible sources of carbohydrate. A larger, more substantial meal should be consumed three to four hours before the event, while a smaller meal or snack should be consumed two hours before. Timing and meal selection prior to the event will depend on individual preference and appetite, as well as the start time of the event. Fat in the meal will slow digestion, and excess fibre should be avoided in order to avoid gastro-intestinal discomfort. Most importantly, the meal should consist of familiar foods with which the athlete feels comfortable. Adequate fluid intake is also essential. An athlete too nervous to eat may prefer a liquid meal such as Gatorpro, Sustagen, Exceed Sports Meal Plus, Ensure or some other low fat milk drink such as a banana 'smoothie'.

Eating one hour pre-event

Intake of carbohydrates in the hour before competition has been reported in some studies to give rise to an 'insulin-mediated rebound hypoglycaemia' (a sudden increase in blood sugar followed by a rapid decrease below normal blood sugar levels), increased glycogen oxidation, reduced use of free fatty acids and the possibility of impaired endurance performance. It appears that while there may be individual variations in response, the possible disadvantages may have been overstated. Individuals who are sensitive to changes to blood glucose levels in the hour before exercise should avoid concentrated sources of carbohydrates (e.g. softdrinks, fruit juices and commercial meal supplements).

Recent research suggests that consuming carbohydrates such as sports drinks or confectionery 5–10 minutes before an event may prolong endurance performance. This practice should be tested in training to avoid possible gastro-intestinal discomfort during competition. Further research is required in this area.

DURING EXERCISE

Carbohydrate and fluid intake is essential during many endurance and ultraendurance events to prevent muscle glycogen depletion, hypoglycaemia (low blood sugar levels) and dehydration. Important factors to consider when consuming food and fluid during an event include:

- Liquid or solid? Athletes should experiment in training with both liquid sources (sports drinks, dilute cordials, glucose syrups such as Leppins) and food sources (e.g. sports bars, bananas) of carbohydrate to determine combinations that suit them best.
- Carbohydrate requirements. The amount of carbohydrate required per hour is influenced by the size of the athlete and by exercise intensity. Carbohydrate requirements, approximately 0.8–1.0g per kilogram of body weight per hour of exercise, are increased with high intensity exercise when muscle glycogen is relied upon more heavily.
- Timing. Foods and fluids should be consumed early to help preserve valuable muscle glycogen stores and maintain optimal hydration status.

Table 8.10: Examples of 50 gram carbohydrate drinks and snacks

750 ml sports drink (e.g. Isosport, Gatorade, Exceed Fluid and Energy
  Replacement, Powerade, Sport Plus)
750 ml cordial
500ml juice or non-cola soft drink
250–400ml Sustagen, Ensure, Exceed Sport Meal or reduced fat
  milkshake/smoothie
1 serve of Gatorpro or Exceed Sport Meal Plus
200–250ml 'carbo-loader' drink (e.g. Gatorlode or Exceed High Carbohydrate Source)
50 grams jelly beans or other jelly lollies
1 round of thick jam/honey/banana sandwiches
3 pieces of fruit
2–3 muesli bars
1 sports bar (e.g., Power Bar, Exceed Sports Bar)
Bowl of cereal with reduced fat milk and banana
Bowl of fruit salad and 200g tub of fruit yoghurt
2 large pancakes with lots of syrup
Bowl of pasta/rice with low fat toppings

- Type of carbohydrate. Easily digestible (low fibre) and convenient carbohydrate foods (e.g. sports bars, bananas, some breakfast bars) are best tolerated and most practical for the athlete to consume during exercise.

During endurance events such as cycling or iron man length triathlons, the athlete must consume fluid as well as carbohydate during the race. A fluid intake of approximately 800–1200 ml per hour and a carbohydrate intake of approximately 50 grams per hour is recommended. Team players should aim to drink 800–1400 ml/hr for males and 600–1000 ml/hr for females during a match. The amount required will vary according to a number of factors, including temperature and humidity, body size, activity level and initial hydration status. Carbohydrate-containing drinks (e.g. sports drinks, dilute cordial) should be considered for use, particularly in situations where matches are scheduled close together or exercise continues for more than 60–90 minutes. Snacks and fluids that provide 50 grams of carbohydrate suitable for consumption during a race are listed in Table 8.10.

RECOVERY

Recovery, discussed in more detail in Chapter 6, should be considered an integral part of every training program and competition routine. Optimal nutritional recovery involves refuelling muscle and liver glycogen stores, repairing muscle damage and replacing fluids and electrolytes lost in sweat.

Refuelling muscle and liver glycogen stores

Athletes should replace approximately 1.0 gram of carbohydrate per kilogram of their body weight (about 50–100 grams) in the first 30 minutes after exercise, and again every 2 hours until the usual daily intake is reached. The 50 gram carbohydrate drinks and snacks listed in Table 8.10 are also ideal for post-exercise recovery.

The fastest rate of recovery is achieved by consuming food and drinks with a moderate-to-high glycaemic index. Examples of these are sports drinks, glucose confectionery, cordials and soft drinks (non-caffeine), fruits such as watermelon and bananas, bread, potatoes and some wheat based breakfast cereals. Inclusion of some fructose (fruit) assists in the replacement of liver glycogen stores. Liquids are generally preferred immediately following exercise. As tolerated by individuals, nutritious carbohydrate foods should be consumed to further replenish muscle and liver glycogen stores.

Repairing muscle damage

Because muscle damage delays glycogen building, carbohydrate replacement is even more crucial when an athlete is injured. For the first few days after an injury, slightly larger serves of protein may also be included in the diet to aid recovery and maintenance of lean body tissue (muscle). Adequate intake of other nutrients such as vitamins, minerals and trace elements will normally be provided in the meals following competition.

The athlete who has suffered a soft tissue injury should avoid drinking alcohol immediately following a match or competition, as alcohol will delay the repair and recovery process to the muscle. The injured athlete should ideally avoid alcohol for the next 24 hours, and should ensure that all carbohydrate and fluid needs are met during this time.

Replacing fluids and electrolytes lost in sweat

Water is an essential nutrient for the athlete; failure to replace fluid losses during exercise results in dehydration. In practical terms this may lead, in both speed and endurance athletes, to fatigue, muscle cramps, inability to control body temperature (overheating), loss of concentration, headaches and gastric upset. All of these result in suboptimal performance. Quite apart from the adverse influence dehydration has on training and playing performance, failure to rehydrate during exercise may be fatal.

Thirst is a poor indicator of fluid needs, particularly for young athletes, and since an individual may lose up to 2–3 litres of fluid during exercise, especially in warmer climates and in the summer months, adequate hydration is a serious concern. Electrolytes (sodium and potassium) are also lost in sweat, but as individuals improve their fitness, these nutrients are better conserved by the kidneys as the sweat becomes more dilute. Athletes do not need to consume extra salt except when they exercise in hot environmental conditions for lengthy periods of time. Additional salt is not required for muscle cramps—in fact, taking in extra salt is more likely to increase the risk of getting cramps.

Athletes should avoid consuming excess caffeine throughout the day (e.g. tea, coffee, cocoa and cola), as it may lead to dehydration. Up to four cups of these beverages per day is a reasonable limit. Alcohol is also a potent diuretic (i.e. causes fluid loss), and for this reason alone should be avoided following exercise while fluid and carbohydrate are replaced. After exercise fluid lost in sweat must be replaced. A kilogram of weight loss during exercise is roughly equal to a litre of fluid that needs to be replaced.

In most exercise situations it is difficult for the athlete to completely replace all fluid losses, for a variety of reasons. These include:

- The availability of fluid—access to fluid during training and competition may be limited.
- Opportunity to drink—rules of a game may restrict fluid intake.

- Gastro-intestinal tolerance to fluid intake while exercising (e.g. in hot, humid environments, fluid needs will often exceed the athlete's maximal fluid intake).
- Awareness of sweat losses (e.g. when cycling, sweat evaporates as quickly as it forms; the athlete is therefore often unaware of sweat losses).
- Tradition within a sport—poor fluid practices within a sport are often passed on from one generation of players to the next.
- Body weight/fat fears—in some sports weight loss during exercise is encouraged.

Fluid intake should begin immediately after exercise, and the athlete must be conscious of continuing replacement over the following 24 hours. The best choices include water, sports drinks (e.g. Isosport, Gatorade, Exceed), carbohydrate loading drinks (e.g. Gatorlode, Exceed Hi-carb), cordials, non-cola soft drinks, and meal replacement/milk drinks (e.g. Sustagen, Exceed Sports Meal, low-fat milk smoothie). The controlled level of electrolytes in sports drinks enhances absorption from the intestines, while cool beverages are more refreshing and palatable.

Practical guidelines to ensure adequate fluid and electrolyte replacement include:

- Hydrating before exercise (i.e. consuming regular drinks all day and up to/during the hour prior to training or competition).
- Ensuring that urine is clear and dilute before exercise.
- Drinking small volumes of fluid (up to 250 ml) at 15–20 minute intervals during exercise where practical.
- Weighing before and after exercise and taking in approximately 1 litre of fluid for every kilogram of weight lost.
- Consuming cool fluids. Water is sufficient for exercise sessions of up to 60–90 minutes.
- Drinking sports drinks containing 5–7% carbohydrate (e.g. glucose or glucose polymers) and low levels of electrolytes for longer training sessions and events. These replace fluids and carbohydrates most effectively.

The choice made by an individual athlete or team may depend on taste preference, cost and availability. A range of carbohydrate drinks may be used to replace fluids and other nutrients after exercise.

DIETARY SUPPLEMENTS AND NUTRITIONAL ERGOGENIC AIDS

All athletes, from the recreational athlete to the professional sportsperson, continually search for ways to increase their sporting performance. Special foods, supplements and con-coctions are often used in an attempt to gain an edge over other competitors. This has resulted in a billion dollar industry which produces 'wonder substances' that provide the 'winning edge'.

Many sport scientists, related health professionals, coaches and athletes confuse dietary supplements with nutritional ergogenic aids. A dietary supplement can be described as a product that contains nutrients in similar amounts to the Recommended Dietary Intakes (RDIs), or contains large amounts of a particular nutrient in order to treat a known nutritional deficiency. They include sports drinks (e.g. Isosport, Gatorade, Sport Plus, Exceed Fluid and Energy Replacement), high carbohydrate supplements (e.g. Gatorlode Relode, Exceed High Carbohydrate Drink Source), liquid meal supplements (e.g. Sustagen Sport, Exceed Sports Meal), sports bars (e.g. Power Bar, Exceed Sports Bar), and vitamin/mineral supplements (e.g. broad range multi-vitamin and iron supplements). Dietary supplements are used by the athlete to meet a nutritional need that usually arises from the added demands of training and competition.

An ergogenic aid, however, by definition is a product or formulation that directly enhances work output or exercise performance. These products often contain nutrients or other substances in large amounts and aim to enhance performance by a drug-like effect.

Popular ergogenic (performance enhancing) aids

Bicarbonate: Bicarbonate loading is thought to improve anaerobic exercise performance, by increasing the buffering capacity of the muscle. As mentioned in Chapter 2, the production of lactic acid (hydrogen ions) is thought to be a limiting factor to performance in high intensity exercise. Athletes competing in events lasting 1–8 minutes (e.g. 200–400m swimming, 800–1500m running, 2000m rowing, 500m and 1000m kayaking) may benefit from ingesting 0.3g of sodium bicarbonate per kilogram of body weight (dissolved in a liquid), 1 or 2 hours before exercise. Numerous well-controlled laboratory studies suggest that ingestion of sodium bicarbonate will reduce the sensation of fatigue at a standard level of exercise, and increasing performance in high intensity anaerobic exercise to exhaustion. For some athletes, however, sodium bicarbonate loading may cause gastro-intestinal distress, including nausea and diarrhoea.

Creatine: Creatine loading for athletes involved in maximal short duration exercise has provoked recent interest within the scientific community. Creatine phosphate is best known for its role in providing a readily available and rapidly released energy source in short, explosive exercise lasting 1–10 seconds (e.g. repeated sprints in team sports, throwing events, sprint running and swimming). Creatine phosphate also plays a role in lactate-producing exercises (as a buffer to lactic acid) and endurance aerobic exercise (as a transporter of high energy phosphate molecules within the muscle).

It has been demonstrated that ingestion of 20g/day of creatine (4 x 5g doses) for 5 days can produce, on average, a 20% increase in muscle creatine. In comparison, dietary sources of creatine (e.g. meats, fish) provide about 1–2g per day for the average adult. It appears that subjects with the lowest initial muscle creatine levels (e.g. vegetarians are reported to have low muscle creatine stores) will benefit most from creatine loading, but continual high doses (e.g. 20g) of creatine will have minimal additional benefit because muscle has an upper limit for creatine storage. Recent findings suggest that work output is significantly increased in repeated bouts of maximal exercise, but minimal evidence exists supporting possible performance benefits during sub-maximal exercise.

Caffeine: The physiological effects of caffeine are well known and include stimulation of the central nervous system, muscle and adrenalin, and diuresis (increased urination). Caffeine is found in a variety of foods and drinks, with major dietary sources (tea, coffee and cola drinks) providing about 30–100mg of caffeine per serve. It has been suggested that caffeine improves endurance performance by stimulating fat metabolism, thus sparing muscle glycogen stores. Research indicates that a 300–500mg dose of caffeine consumed within the hour before exercise may prevent early fatigue. Caffeine intake during the event may further improve performance by stimulating the nervous system, masking the effects of fatigue.

Since research indicates a wide variety of individual responses to caffeine intake, athletes should experiment during training to determine potential performance benefits. It should be remembered that caffeine intakes in the order of 500mg or above may cause urinary caffeine levels above the legal level as specified by the International Olympic Committee.

Glycerol has recently captured the attention of many sport scientists, coaches and endurance athletes. A major goal for the endurance athlete during exercise, particularly in the heat, is to maintain an adequate hydration level. A glycerol intake of approximately 1g of glycerol and 20–25ml of water per kilogram of body weight, prior to exercise, induces hyperhydration (fluid retention). It has been reported that glycerol-induced hyperhydration may reduce the thermal stress of exercise in the heat and in turn improve endurance performance. Although research has provided moderate support for an ergogenic effect of glycerol-induced hyperhydration in endurance events, further research is required to determine mechanisms of action.

In summary, nutrition plays a central role in both training and performance. It is entirely possible that the fittest athlete or player can lose an event or game due to inadequate attention to nutritional preparation and recovery from a previous exercise session. Clearly, failure to recognise the importance of dietary practices in the overall scheme of performance will prevent an athlete from reaching full potential.

SUMMARY

- The diet must provide adequate energy, be consistent with long-term eating habits, promote optimal performance during competition and enhance recovery following exercise.
- Carbohydrates supply the glycogen which allows muscles to maintain a high rate of contraction. An insufficient amount of carbohydrates in the diet will accelerate the fatigue process and slow down recovery.
- A balanced diet will provide an adequate intake of protein. The current position taken by sports science is that the majority of athletes gain no physiological advantage from protein supplements.
- Fat loss is best achieved by combining endurance training with a low-fat diet. Bulking up is best achieved by having several small meals a day and ensuring that training is supported by a high carbohydrate diet.
- Following exercise, drinking fluids to rehydrate and the replenishment of the body's carbohydate stores must be the athlete's highest nutritional priorities.

RECOMMENDED READING

Burke, L. (1992) *The Complete Guide to Food for Sports Performance*, Allen & Unwin, Sydney; 2nd edn 1995.

Burke, L., and V. Deakin, (eds) (1994) *Clinical Sports Nutrition*, McGraw-Hill, Sydney.

Costill, D.L., and M. Hargreaves, (1992) 'Carbohydrate nutrition and fatigue', *Sports Medicine*, 13 (2): 86–92.

'Proceedings of the Gatorade Sports Science Institute Conference on Nutritional Ergogenic Aids', (1995) *International Journal of Sport Nutrition*, 5: S1-S131.

Sherman, W.M., and G.S. Wimer, (1991) 'Insufficient dietary carbohydrate during training: does it impair athletic performance?' *International Journal of Sport Nutrition*. 1: 28–44.

Williams, M.H., (1995) 'Nutritional ergogenics in athletics' *Journal of Sports Sciences*, 13: S63-S74.

Index